MW01379595

The
LORD
and
Money

Commentaries by Clayton Lindemuth

Hardgrave Enterprises
CHESTERFIELD, MO

Clayton Lindemuth/Hardgrave Enterprises
15470-3 Elk Ridge Lane
Chesterfield, MO 63017

Book Layout ©2013 BookDesignTemplates.com

Cover Photo by Marcin Wichary. No changes made to photo except cropping. Creative Commons license https://creativecommons.org/licenses/by/2.0/legalcode

The LORD and Money/Clayton Lindemuth. -- 1st ed.
ISBN: 978-0692215371

Dedicated to:

Pastor Dave Desforge

Pastor Mark Martin

But seek ye first the kingdom of God, and his righteousness; and all these things shall be added unto you.

−MATTHEW 6:33

Table of Contents

Introduction

I've heard that it's important to start a presentation with information that is important to everyone, so let me paraphrase one of my favorite pastors, Mark Martin, from Phoenix Arizona: *I've read the Bible to the end and I don't want spoil it for you, but everything turns out good.*

We win.

But in the meantime we have to navigate the world in which we find ourselves, where not everything seems to turn out the way we might like.

My hope is that while reading this book you'll be moved to believe as I do, that although God doesn't promise us prosperity, He has ordered the world so that several kinds of wealth often result from keeping Him first and following His advice.

I don't want to spend much time talking about myself because I'm not going to ask you to trust me based on my authority as an expert. As in all things relating to faith, I believe we're duty bound to think for ourselves, refer to the information God gave us to help make sense of the world, and consult Him directly on a regular basis.

I came to Christ in the year 2000. Friedrich Nietzsche's aphorisms are cute and aggressive and well suited to rebel teenagers, but once you get older you need more substance. I grew up being the black sheep amidst three Christian friends, so I wasn't completely unfamiliar with Christianity. But it didn't fit a Big Bang and evolution kind of world.

By the time I was thirty my wife and I were introduced to Grace Church in Asheville, North Carolina, and Pastor Dave Desforge introduced me to *The Case for Christ* by Lee Strobel. I read everything Strobel wrote, and that turned into a fascination with apologetics, which eventually led me to an intellectual belief that Christ was born, crucified, and resurrected, and even that it was on account of my personal sin.

But I had no relationship. That didn't happen until I lost my wedding ring making pizza dough. I replaced it with another that had First Thessalonians 5:17, PRAY WITHOUT CEASING inscribed in Greek.

I started praying without ceasing, and what I prayed was, "God do something about my work. I hate my job." I went in to work a few days later and became unemployed, which is an uncanny way to start a true relationship with Christ... but not really if you think about it.

Because as long as we think we can do everything ourselves, we don't need Him. But when we're on our knees, humbled, we find He's standing beside us.

I started talking to Him frequently and a few months later, Pastor Mark Martin baptized me.

During the fifteen years I've been helping people with their financial lives, I've found they also get their financial information from Uncle Bob, the television, and salespeople—but rarely the Bible.

On the other hand, I noticed that there are a lot of folks giving financial advice who use scripture out of context to support questionable and sometimes self-serving advice, or bend the Bible to modern notions of financial planning, as if modern finance is the standard to which God must adapt.

In reality, the Bible doesn't contain a single word about fifteen year mortgages, mutual funds, or term life insurance. Nor did Jesus say, "I promise you material wealth if you just write enough checks to the church."

I suppose that might be why we don't often turn to the Bible for advice about money.

It's almost as if the modern world is so complex that the Bible is hopelessly outdated. That there's no way to live in today's fast paced and confusing economic world using a guide book that was written thousands of years ago.

But I'm going to show you that the terrain you have to navigate is really just made up of God, human beings, and markets, and though the Old Covenant and the New Covenant have changed our relationship with God, which has in turn made obsolete some of the Old Testament promises about material prosperity, our relationships with other human beings haven't changed at all, and Bible's advice about money ultimately leads to financial health today just as it did four thousand years ago.

The practical advice of the bible is just as relevant today as it was in the time of Moses.

This is a short preamble before we get started with a little bit of theology.

What is economics? Everything. Human action, labor, markets, savings, investment, risk, relationships. Everything in the bible can be understood through an economic prism.

Think of this: *the wages of sin is death.* Does that mean that a person's job is sin and his payment is death?

Imagine you're at work and the boss comes up and says, hey, we're no longer paying you twenty dollars an hour. Now, each time you assemble that part, we kill you.

You'd stop working, right?

The wages of sin is death. The verse works on a couple levels.

Wages are a contractual benefit paid out to compensate us for our work. And if our work is evil, the compensation is death.

But it gets more interesting if we take it a little deeper. If you have a 15 dollar per hour job you don't like, you're free to find another employer who might pay you more.

Your work commands a value based on how much you accomplish, and how much others need what you do. So if you find an employer who really needs what you do, your work might command $20/hour.

Except that in the divine marketplace, if your work is sin, then it has no intrinsic value. In fact, it carries a negative value. You can't go to another marketplace but even if you could, the value of sin is still nothing because it produces nothing worthwhile.

So the wages of sin is death, in an economic sense, means both that sin has no value to God, and that it's actually so bad that the fair compensation is your annihilation.

I'm not suggesting that the divine marketplace, which is really God giving us what we actually deserve, is a perfect parallel to Wall Street markets, but it does create an obvious point of comparison.

Markets can be unkind. They can be harsh, and we may not get something we think is fair in exchange for our work.

And since the entire world is a place where we do things and there are effects, which we either call rewards or consequences depending on how much we like them, the entire world is a kind of marketplace. We don't always get what we want or believe is fair.

The Bible is doubly interesting because it tells us not just how to get the best result in the divine marketplace, but also in the human marketplace.

The wisdom is meant for both our souls and our lives in a fallen world.

You'll see as we go forward that the idea of an exchange is ever present. Every piece of wisdom fits into one category or another: God telling us how to get along with Him, how to be holy, or God telling us how to get along with other human beings, how to live in a fallen world.

In fact, the premise of this book is that the world is ordered such that when we follow God's advice on money, on average, we do pretty well.

That doesn't mean that God promises everyone is going to be rich, or that you can avoid sickness or tragedy, or tithe your way to prosperity.

Only that God's rules for personal finance happen to work, and if you have an average life and apply God's advice on money, you'll have above average wealth.

1   Rules for Interpreting Scripture

Theologians and scholars have established principles for interpreting scripture to help reduce the likelihood that God's word will be misunderstood or misapplied. We've all seen instances of someone quoting scripture, getting it wrong, and twisting the meaning. We've also all seen scripture removed from context that lends important insight into the meaning of the scripture. Sometimes it's obvious, but other times, less so.

In addition, we all run the risk of reading scripture we don't want to read, and then seeking some alternate way to understand it so we don't have to change our beliefs or confront aspects of our personalities or behaviors that we don't want to confront. Thus it's good to have consistent rules for interpreting scripture.

First find the definition of the words or terms that you're considering, and then stay true to the definition. The meaning of a word or term should be established according to the common definition of the people who spoke the language when the passage was written, with a preference for simple, everyday meanings, not obscure ones.

Don't take words or terms out of context. Many words depend on context for meaning, and context should be understood to include insights gleaned from the history of when the passage was written.

Don't interpret words or phrases in ways that are illogical given the overall premise. On whole, there should be a consistency of meaning across an entire document.

Last, try to avoid making grand leaps in understanding based on feelings or intuition. The Bible exists so that we may know God; it only makes sense to prefer interpretations that are accessible, rather than convoluted or obscure.

2 Old Covenant and New Covenant

Deuteronomy 28: 1-6

And it shall come to pass, if thou shalt hearken diligently unto the voice of the LORD thy God, to observe and to do all his commandments which I command thee this day, that the LORD thy God will set thee on high above all nations of the earth: And all these blessings shall come on thee, and overtake thee, if thou shalt hearken unto the voice of the LORD thy God. Blessed shalt thou be in the city, and blessed shalt thou be in the field. Blessed shall be the fruit of thy body, and the fruit of thy ground, and the fruit of thy cattle, the increase of thy kine, and the flocks of thy sheep. Blessed shall be thy basket and thy store. Blessed shalt thou be when thou comest in, and blessed shalt thou be when thou goest out.

Jeremiah 31: 31-34

Behold, the days come, saith the LORD, that I will make a new covenant with the house of Israel, and with the house of Judah: Not according to the covenant that I made with their fathers in the day that I took them by the hand to bring them out of the land of Egypt; which my covenant they brake, although I was an husband unto them, saith the LORD: But this shall be the covenant that I will make with the house of Israel; **After those days, saith the LORD, I will put my law in their inward parts, and write it in their hearts; and will be their God, and they shall be my people.** And they shall teach no more every man his neighbour, and every man his brother, saying, Know the LORD: for they shall all know me, from the least of them unto the greatest of them, saith the LORD: for I will forgive their iniquity, and I will remember their sin no more.

John 3: 16

For God so loved the world, that he gave his only begotten Son, that whosoever believeth in him should not perish, but have everlasting life.

Hebrews 9: 11-15

But Christ being come an high priest of good things to come, by a greater and more perfect tabernacle, not made with hands, that is to say, not of this building; Neither by the blood of goats and calves, but by his own blood he entered in once into the holy place, having obtained eternal redemption for us. For if the blood of bulls and of goats, and the ashes of an heifer sprinkling the unclean, sanctifieth to the purifying of the flesh: How much more shall the blood of Christ, who through the eternal Spirit offered himself without spot to God, purge your conscience from dead works to serve the living God? And for this cause he is the mediator of the new testament, that by means of death, for the redemption of the transgressions that were under the first testament, they which are called might receive the promise of eternal inheritance.

Romans 6: 23

For the wages of sin is death; but the gift of God is eternal life through Jesus Christ our Lord.

Hebrews 8: 13

In that he saith, a new covenant, he hath made the first old. Now that which decayeth and waxeth old is ready to vanish away.

Commentary

The Old Covenant was an accord between two parties, the Hebrews and God. The people were to honor the Lord by keeping His laws, and their reward as stated in Deuteronomy 28 was that the Lord would bless their towns, children, fields, flocks, fruit baskets, breadboards, going in and coming out. Everything. When they saw others prosper, it was natural to assume God blessed them.

However, human beings are not perfect—and because the Lord is just, He cannot tolerate sin. The penalty of sin is death.

Yet, because God loved his chosen people, he permitted them to sacrifice a cherished or valuable animal in their place. The Lord intended the penalty be painful, so that people would understand that sin has consequences. The Old Covenant erected an entire structure for dealing with human sin that was essentially God allowing us to substitute an animal in place of ourselves, so that we would associate blood and death with sin, and learn not to do it.

Even under the Old Covenant, God was pointing forward and telling the people that he would someday make a new Covenant with them, and Jeremiah 31: 33 is very important:

> I will put my instructions deep within them, and I will write them on their hearts.

One of the most basic understandings of the Christian worldview is that before Christ, God the Father accepted animal sacrifice to atone for sins, but that was a temporary situation. In Christ, God the Father gave a perfect sacrifice on behalf of all of us, and the only thing we have to do to receive the gift of salvation is to believe it.

Hebrews makes the transition from blood sacrifice to Christ's sacrifice plain.

Because Christ suffered and died to atone for our sins, our debts are paid. What is required of us is that we place our faith in Christ. When we acknowledge Him as our Savior, He bestows through grace the gift of forgiveness. His sacrificial death becomes our atonement.

It's interesting to think of this in economic terms for a moment. The reason our salvation is a gift is that there is nothing we could possibly do to earn it.

Meaning both that God is **so** holy we can't even get close enough to barter a trade with Him, and our works can't possibly accumulate enough value to be a fair exchange for the Son of God's suffering.

Our faith in Christ alone saves us, thus we are no longer required to keep the law or sacrifice animals to atone for sin. Instead, when we place our faith in Christ, the Holy Spirit enters our hearts—and that's what the previous scripture refers to, God writing His instructions on our hearts.

The indwelling Spirit of God replaces the laws of the Old Covenant, and we turn to the Spirit, not law, for guidance. The Old Testament law is still a profoundly good resource for understanding what is likely to please the Lord. Also, the outcomes of keeping the law—many of which are simply the natural rewards of sensible, clean living—are the same, but because we are followers of Christ, the penalty for failing to keep the law has been paid.

Hebrews 8:13 makes it perfectly plain that the Old Covenant is no longer operative:

> "When God speaks of a "new" covenant, it means
> he has made the first one obsolete."

We can't make a sacrifice and expect that God will say okay we're even. The only way forward is through the New Covenant, Jesus Christ.

Something that is important to remember is that whenever you read scripture where God promises prosperity, you have to look and see whether it's under the Old Covenant or not. Because that arrangement is obsolete.

The lines we just reviewed from Deuteronomy 28, about blessing us coming and going, wherever we go and whatever we do, were part of the Old Covenant. Thus, obedience to the Law of Moses doesn't obligate God to prospering you.

Instead, under the New Covenant, we're new creations, and we're given a new way of following God's will.

> Therefore, if anyone is in Christ, he is a new creation. —2 Corinthians 5:17

Under the Old Covenant, we were the same old human beings, but system of priests and animal sacrifices gave us a temporary way of cleansing our sins. But under the New Covenant, we are new creations.

The way that God transforms us into new beings is by changing the way we think.

> "Don't copy the behavior and customs of this world, but let God transform you into a new person by changing the way you think. Then you will learn to know God's will for you, which is good and pleasing and perfect. —Romans 12:2

If you've read any self-help literature of the last few decades, you know that if you sow a thought, you reap an action. The result of God transforming our thoughts is that we behave differently.

Our focus should be building relationship with the Lord, and behaving as the indwelling Spirit of God directs us. We should pray, study the Bible, and enjoy fellowship with other Christians. If we do this, we will find the insights we need to keep us on a godly path.

Our works, which include how we treat other people with love and compassion, give evidence of our walk with the Lord.

3   Works result from Faith

2 Corinthians 5:17

Therefore if any man be in Christ, he is a new creature: old things are passed away; behold, all things are become new.

Romans 12:1-2

I beseech you therefore, brethren, by the mercies of God, that ye present your bodies a living sacrifice, holy, acceptable unto God, which is your reasonable service. **And be not conformed to this world: but be ye transformed by the renewing of your mind, that ye may prove what is that good, and acceptable, and perfect, will of God.**

John 15: 1-8

I am the true vine, and my Father is the husbandman. Every branch in me that beareth not fruit he taketh away: and every branch that beareth fruit, he purgeth it, that it may bring forth more fruit. Now ye are clean through the word which I have spoken unto you. Abide in me, and I in you. As the branch cannot bear fruit of itself, except it abide in the vine; no more can ye, except ye abide in me. **I am the vine, ye are the branches: He that abideth in me, and I in him, the same bringeth forth much fruit: for without me ye can do nothing.** If a man abide not in me, he is cast forth as a branch, and is withered; and men gather them, and cast them into the fire, and they are burned. If ye abide in me, and my words abide in you, ye shall ask what ye will, and it shall be done unto you. Herein is my Father glorified, that ye bear much fruit; so shall ye be my disciples.

James 1: 21-27

Wherefore lay apart all filthiness and superfluity of naughtiness, and receive with meekness the engrafted word, which is able to save your souls. But be ye doers of the word, and not hearers only, deceiving your own selves. For if any be a hearer of the word, and not a doer, he is like unto a man beholding his natural face in a glass: For he beholdeth himself, and goeth his way, and straightway forgetteth what manner of man he was. But whoso looketh into the perfect law of liberty, and continueth therein, he being not a forgetful hearer, but a doer of the work, this man shall be blessed in his deed. If any man among you seem to be religious, and bridleth not his tongue, but deceiveth his own heart, this man's religion is vain. Pure religion and undefiled before God and the Father is this, to visit the fatherless and widows in their affliction, and to keep himself unspotted from the world.

James 2: 14-18

What doth it profit, my brethren, though a man say he hath faith, and have not works? can faith save him? If a brother or sister be naked, and destitute of daily food, And one of you say unto them, Depart in peace, be ye warmed and filled; notwithstanding ye give them not those things which are needful to the body; what doth it profit? Even so faith, if it hath not works, is dead, being alone. Yea, a man may say, Thou hast faith, and I have works: shew me thy faith without thy works, and I will shew thee my faith by my works.

1 John 2: 15, 16

Love not the world, neither the things that are in the world. If any man love the world, the love of the Father is not in him. For all that is in the world, the lust of the flesh, and the lust of the eyes, and the pride of life, is not of the Father, but is of the world.

Romans 8:6-11

For to be carnally minded is death; but to be spiritually minded is life and peace. Because the carnal mind is enmity against God: for it is not subject to the law of God, neither indeed can be. So then they that are in the flesh cannot please God. But ye are not in the flesh, but in the Spirit, if so be that the Spirit of God dwell in you. Now if any man have not the Spirit of Christ, he is none of his. And if Christ be in you, the body is dead because of sin; but the Spirit is life because of righteousness. But if the Spirit of him that raised up Jesus from the dead dwell in you, he that raised up Christ from the dead shall also quicken your mortal bodies by his Spirit that dwelleth in you.

Commentary

The evidence of walking with the Lord is that He moves us to be more like Him. We become more aware of right and wrong, and He gives us desires like His: to love, to help, to forgive. As Christ says in John 15,

> "A branch cannot produce fruit if it is severed from the vine, and you cannot be fruitful unless you remain in me."

We desire to honor the Father, and become deeply moved for our fellow human beings.

In John 15: 7, where Christ says,

> You may ask for anything you want and it will be granted...

This is within the specific context of producing fruit, which refers back to Christ being the vine and us being the branches.

Fruit is not material wealth. It is the work of God, and what this passage means is that if you are truly doing God's work you can expect his full help. It doesn't mean that if you're a Christian and you want to win the lottery, you should just ask.

In James 1:21 we find the key:

> Humbly accept the word God has planted in our hearts, for it has the power to save our souls.

When the Spirit of God enters us, we learn to rely on the Lord not just for our salvation, but to guide our desires and ambitions.

One of the first things He does is make us understand in our hearts what is actually good and pleasing to God. James 1:27 tells us that we will know what is right because God will tell us, and so we better make sure to do what God says.

> Pure and genuine religion in the sight of God the Father means caring for orphans and widows in their distress and refusing to let the world corrupt us.

So to put everything together that we've discussed so far, under the Old Covenant, human beings were given a law book to follow, and if they followed all the laws, they could expect to be blessed by God, and it was natural to equate economic success with virtue.

Then all the rules changed with Christ. Instead of having laws to follow, we now have the indwelling Spirit of God guiding us, which transforms the way we think, makes God's will known to us in our hearts, and gives us the challenge of actually living up to what we know is right.

The obvious question, then, is if you are a Christian and you are totally possessed by a desire to create wealth—do you think that desire is coming from you, or from the indwelling Spirit of God?

1 John 2 says:

> When you love the world, you do not have the love of the Father in you.

It seems pretty clear that if wealth is going to occur to a person who is absolutely right with God, it can't be because it was that person's highest objective, because that would replace the will of God and all of God's priorities.

But does that mean Godly people shouldn't care about their finances? Or that they should just expect to be poor?

4 Rely on the LORD

Deuteronomy 5: 6-10

I am the LORD thy God, which brought thee out of the land of Egypt, from the house of bondage. **Thou shalt have none other gods before me**. Thou shalt not make thee any graven image, or any likeness of any thing that is in heaven above, or that is in the earth beneath, or that is in the waters beneath the earth: Thou shalt not bow down thyself unto them, nor serve them: for I the LORD thy God am a jealous God, visiting the iniquity of the fathers upon the children unto the third and fourth generation of them that hate me, And shewing mercy unto thousands of them that love me and keep my commandments

Exodus 16:19-21

And Moses said, Let no man leave of it till the morning. Notwithstanding they hearkened not unto Moses; but some of them left of it until the morning, and it bred worms, and stank: and Moses was wroth with them. And they gathered it every morning, every man according to his eating: and when the sun waxed hot, it melted.

Moses said to them, "Let no one leave of it [keep manna] until the morning." Notwithstanding **they did not listen to Moses, but some of them left of it until the morning, and it bred worms,** and became foul: and Moses was angry with them. They gathered it morning by morning, everyone according to his eating. When the sun grew hot, it melted. It happened that on the sixth day they gathered twice as much bread, two omers for each one, and all the rulers of the congregation came and told Moses. He said to them, "This is that which the LORD has spoken, **'Tomorrow is a solemn rest, a holy Sabbath to the LORD. Bake that which you want to bake, and boil that which you want to boil; and all that remains over lay up for yourselves to be kept until the morning.'"**

Matthew 6:11

Give us this day our daily bread.

Leviticus 25:21-22

Then I will command my blessing upon you in the sixth year, and it shall bring forth fruit for three years. And ye shall sow the eighth year, and eat yet of old fruit until the ninth year; until her fruits come in ye shall eat of the old store.

Matthew 6:19-34

Lay not up for yourselves treasures upon earth, where moth and rust doth corrupt, and where thieves break through and steal: But lay up for yourselves treasures in heaven, where neither moth nor rust doth corrupt, and where thieves do not break through nor steal: For where your treasure is, there will your heart be also. The light of the body is the eye: if therefore thine eye be single, thy whole body shall be full of light. But if thine eye be evil, thy whole body shall be full of darkness. If therefore the light that is in thee be darkness, how great is that darkness! No man can serve two masters: for either he will hate the one, and love the other; or else he will hold to the one, and despise the other. Ye cannot serve God and mammon. Therefore I say unto you, Take no thought for your life, what ye shall eat, or what ye shall drink; nor yet for your body, what ye shall put on. Is not the life more than meat, and the body than raiment. Behold the fowls of the air: for they sow not, neither do they reap, nor gather into barns; yet your heavenly Father feedeth them. Are ye not much better than they? Which of you by taking thought can add one cubit unto his stature? And why take ye thought for raiment? Consider the lilies of the field, how they grow; they toil not, neither do they spin: And yet I say unto you, That even Solomon in all his glory was not arrayed like one of these. Wherefore, if God so clothe the grass of the field, which to day is, and to morrow is cast into the oven, shall he not much more clothe you, O ye of little faith? Therefore take no thought, saying, What shall we eat? or, What shall we drink? or, Wherewithal shall we be clothed? (For after all these things do the Gentiles seek:) for your heavenly Father knoweth that ye have need of all these things. But seek ye first the kingdom of God, and his righteousness; and all these things shall be added unto you. Take therefore no thought for the morrow: for the morrow shall take thought for the things of itself. Sufficient unto the day is the evil thereof.

Genesis 14:21-23

And the king of Sodom said unto Abram, Give me the persons, and take the goods to thyself. And Abram said to the king of Sodom, I have lift up mine hand unto the Lord, the most high God, the possessor of heaven and earth, That I will not take from a thread even to a shoelatchet, and that I will not take any thing that is thine, lest thou shouldest say, I have made Abram rich…

2 Kings 4: 1-7

Now there cried a certain woman of the wives of the sons of the prophets unto Elisha, saying, Thy servant my husband is dead; and thou knowest that thy servant did fear the LORD: and the creditor is come to take unto him my two sons to be bondmen. And Elisha said unto her, What shall I do for thee? tell me, what hast thou in the house? And she said, Thine handmaid hath not any thing in the house, save a pot of oil. Then he said, Go, borrow thee vessels abroad of all thy neighbours, even empty vessels; borrow not a few. And when thou art come in, thou shalt shut the door upon thee and upon thy sons, and shalt pour out into all those vessels, and thou shalt set aside that which is full. So she went from him, and shut the door upon her and upon her sons, who brought the vessels to her; and she poured out. And it came to pass, when the vessels were full, that she said unto her son, Bring me yet a vessel. And he said unto her, There is not a vessel more. And the oil stayed. Then she came and told the man of God. And he said, Go, sell the oil, and pay thy debt, and live thou and thy children of the rest.

Mark 4: 18-19

And these are they which are sown among thorns; such as hear the word, And the cares of this world, and the deceitfulness of riches, and the lusts of other things entering in, choke the word, and it becometh unfruitful.

1 Timothy 6:9-11

But they that will be rich fall into temptation and a snare, and into many foolish and hurtful lusts, which drown men in destruction and perdition. For the love of money is the root of all evil: which while some coveted after, they have erred from the faith, and pierced themselves through with many sorrows. But thou, O man of God, flee these things; and follow after righteousness, godliness, faith, love, patience, meekness.

James 1:11

For the sun is no sooner risen with a burning heat, but it withereth the grass, and the flower thereof falleth, and the grace of the fashion of it perisheth: so also shall the rich man fade away in his ways.

Mark 8:36

For what shall it profit a man, if he shall gain the whole world, and lose his own soul?

Ephesians 2: 9-10

Not of works, lest any man should boast. For we are his workmanship, created in Christ Jesus unto good works, which God hath before ordained that we should walk in them.

Commentary:

I.

Although the covenants change from the Old Testament to the New, the Lord is consistent in His desire that His people trust Him to provide. For forty years as the Chosen People wandered the desert, the Lord provided their daily sustenance in the form of manna. As if to stress that they were to depend upon Him and not themselves, they were unable to stockpile manna. It would spoil. However, on the sixth day, manna saved for the Sabbath would not spoil. We are to derive two lessons: the Lord will provide, and the Lord desires that we rest in Him.

The Lord hasn't provided manna for a long time, so how do we trust that he will provide today and tomorrow? What does "the Lord provides" mean in today's world? Is His provision contingent upon something that we must do?

The first consideration is whether we are keeping the Lord first in our lives, or placing other gods before Him. Because we are commanded to keep the Lord first, anything that takes our trust, thoughts, goals, and ambitions away from Him is a false god. Anything in which we place our trust, outside of Him, is a god. Almost anything has the potential to be a god, but one that threatens almost everyone is self-reliance.

If we let go control over our destinies, and trust the Lord to guide the ship, we are free to spend our time in balance with Him, family, charity, work, and ministry. We are free to spend our time where He tells us, and we'll know, because we will be seeking His will and the indwelling Spirit of God will guide us. He might lead us to do anything. The ultimate outcome of our works is for Him alone to decide.

If we don't let go control, but seek to direct our fates, we will deprive ourselves of His direction for our lives. The flesh—our earthly desires—will fill the void left by the absence of God. Because He will not be in our works, we will not have His special provision easing the way, and we will realize that if our goals are to happen, we must assume total responsibility for them. The false god of Self Reliance becomes inevitable when we fail to keep the Lord first in our hearts.

A simple test is whether the objective you're striving for is displacing your relationship with the Lord. If so, it isn't from Him. His first commandment on the stone tablets was having no god before Him. Our first priority should be to cultivate a deep relationship with the Lord. He will provide our second and third and fourth priorities.

Consider the early followers of Christ, who gladly sold their possessions when needed so that there would be no desperate poor among them. They sought the Lord's will and he pointed them in radical directions—for the benefit of glorifying Him and helping to ease the suffering of others. If the Lord is the source of human ambition, it likely will glorify Him and help other people. It will likely demonstrate love, because one of the main task of the Spirit of God is to make us more Christ-like.

The key is the priority of a person's heart. If you pursue a goal the Lord is not telling you to pursue, such as becoming wealthy, you may get your wealth, but you will not have a deep relationship with the Lord. Christ asks, what is it worth to gain the world and lose your soul? If you keep the Lord first, you will have the greatest prize of all. Secondarily, you may be entrusted with wealth or poverty. It is for Him to decide. If it is wealth, however, the works you accomplish with the wealth you have been entrusted with will be quite different than if it was your own ambition that created the wealth. This is a deeper meaning when Christ says it is as difficult for a rich person to go to heaven as a camel through the eye of a needle. It is difficult if the camel has to navigate the eye of the needle himself. Christ continues, however, that all things are possible through God, meaning the rich person who relies on God can make it to heaven. Again, the lesson is about where we keep the Lord in our hearts. Wealth must always be secondary, and that will always mean that for some people, wealth will not be part of the plan. His will be done...

II.

The modern world is fast paced and noisy. We face a barrage of messages vying for our attention, and a thousand demands on our time. We are often in debt before we know what debt is, and finding employment suitable to provide for a family often requires years of education, training, and experience. The hazard is that if we do not seek the Lords will in all things, and instead develop a sense of self-reliance, we might find it easy to justify decisions that lead us farther from the Lord. We study a profession, often going into debt to do so; we gain employment and have to 'work our way up;' or we start a business and have to work all the time. We can easily justify spending evenings until midnight studying our profession. After all, we have families who rely on us. Or our desire to provide for our families can lead to the desire to attain security through the stockpiling wealth.

Further, when we vest total financial responsibility in ourselves, we are inclined to pursue security, because we rightly recognize there will come a day when we will no longer work like we do today. Or we recognize that life is full of hazards that might keep us from our labors—all the more reason to store up wealth. With our wealth we hope to buy security, but the Lord pointed out, we store it where moths, rust, and thieves destroy.

Christ said we cannot serve two masters, both Him and wealth. When we assume ultimate responsibility for our financial wellbeing, we shoulder a heavy yoke. This is why the Lord tells us to consider the lilies and not to worry about security. He will provide. His burden is light.

This does not mean that monetary security is bad, or that acquiring it is evidence of bad living. In fact, other scripture teaches that walking with the Lord includes diligence and good stewardship over what he has entrusted to us, and the results of diligence and good stewardship are the accumulation of wealth. The key is where our priorities lie.

Abram could have kept the goods his men had taken from Sodom, and doing so would have increased his tithe. Increased riches could have allowed him to do more for the poor, or employ the money to a dozen other good purposes. The greatest purpose Abram could spend the money on, however, was that everyone would know the Lord made him rich, not Sodom. In rejecting the spoils, in essence, he spent them on this profound declaration that he kept the Lord first in all things.

III.

A final point on relying on the Lord. When Christ says don't worry about what you'll eat or drink, I think the message here is that you're not alone for your survival on planet earth, and that you should not allow fear over not having necessities warp you into a person who ONLY cares about money or material needs.

> Seek the Kingdom of God above all else, and live righteously, and he will give you everything you need. --Matthew 6:33

The message here is that if you put God first and seek to live righteously, that you'll find the world is ordered such that you'll be okay—either because you work hard, live according to principles that we'll soon get into, and prosper, or because God Himself will reach into our world to take care of you.

I think it's very significant that it isn't just greed that we have to be on the lookout against.

> All too quickly God's message is crowded out by the worries of this life... --Mark 4:18

That means we feel the need to rely on ourselves, and that leads us away from God.

Fear can push us into ungodly behavior as easily as greed. Imagine a person in the park, hungry, homeless and desperate. He sees a man's wallet fall from his pocket as he sits on a park bench… Does the homeless man have to work at controlling his greed, or his fear?

In our financial lives we need to be on guard against fear and worry, not just greed and the desire for wealth.

5 Manipulating the LORD

Acts 8: 9-23

But there was a certain man, called Simon, which before time in the same city used sorcery, and bewitched the people of Samaria, giving out that himself was some great one: To whom they all gave heed, from the least to the greatest, saying, This man is the great power of God. And to him they had regard, because that of long time he had bewitched them with sorceries. But when they believed Philip preaching the things concerning the kingdom of God, and the name of Jesus Christ, they were baptized, both men and women. Then Simon himself believed also: and when he was baptized, he continued with Philip, and wondered, beholding the miracles and signs which were done.

Now when the apostles which were at Jerusalem heard that Samaria had received the word of God, they sent unto them Peter and John: Who, when they were come down, prayed for them, that they might receive the Holy Ghost: (For as yet he was fallen upon none of them: only they were baptized in the name of the Lord Jesus.) Then laid they their hands on them, and they received the Holy Ghost. And when Simon saw that through laying on of the apostles' hands the Holy Ghost was given, he offered them money, Saying, Give me also this power, that on whomsoever I lay hands, he may receive the Holy Ghost. But Peter said unto him, Thy money perish with thee, because thou hast thought that the gift of God may be purchased with money. Thou hast neither part nor lot in this matter: for thy heart is not right in the sight of God. Repent therefore of this thy wickedness, and pray God, if perhaps the thought of thine heart may be forgiven thee. For I perceive that thou art in the gall of bitterness, and in the bond of iniquity.

Proverbs 17: 23

A wicked man taketh a gift out of the bosom to pervert the ways of judgment.

Deuteronomy 10:17

For the LORD your God is God of gods, and Lord of lords, a great God, a mighty, and a terrible, which regardeth not persons, nor taketh reward:

Deuteronomy 16:19

Thou shalt not wrest judgment; thou shalt not respect persons, neither take a gift: for a gift doth blind the eyes of the wise, and pervert the words of the righteous.

Psalm 26:9-10

Gather not my soul with sinners, nor my life with bloody men:[10] In whose hands is mischief, and their right hand is full of bribes.

Ecclesiastes 7:7

Surely oppression maketh a wise man mad; and a gift destroyeth the heart.

Ezekiel 22:12

In thee have they taken gifts to shed blood; thou hast taken usury and increase, and thou hast greedily gained of thy neighbours by extortion, and hast forgotten me, saith the Lord GOD.

Proverbs 3:9-10

Honour the LORD with thy substance, and with the first fruits of all thine increase: So shall thy barns be filled with plenty, and thy presses shall burst out with new wine

Commentary

Simon Magus, the Simon referred to above in Acts, attempted to buy the power of God. The term Simony, derived from his name, refers to paying for the sacraments or attempting to buy an office in the church.

While it is readily apparent that God condemns bribery as a sin, how does that illuminate our understanding of those who tithe in the expectation of receiving material blessings as a reward, or those who pray selfishly?

And to make the question muddier, how are we to read Proverbs 3, which creates a trade-off: honor the Lord with a tithe so your barn will be filled with plenty...

Who is more likely to please the Lord? A person who despises the Lord, ignores what He says, but seeks to win supernatural favor by offering money... or a person who loves the Lord and honors Him by returning a portion of what He provides?

Inherent in the concept of a bribe is that the natural order of things is disrupted. A person transfers something of value to another, and in exchange, the latter exercises power unjustly to favor the former. Bribery is a sin because it disrupts justice.

Is it likely that the absolute Creator of moral values will corrupt them to receive a tithe of something He already owns?

The answer is unequivocally no.

On a similar theme, a craze started with the publication in 2000 of <u>The Prayer of Jabez</u>, by Bruce Wilkinson, who built the book around a few lines in 1 Chronicles 4:9.

> There was a man named Jabez who was more honorable than any of his brothers. His mother named him Jabez because his birth had been so painful. He was the one who prayed to the God of Israel, "Oh,

that you would bless me and expand my territory!
Please be with me in all that I do, and keep me from
all trouble and pain!" And God granted him his re-
quest.

Bruce Wilkinson, the author, in the book said, "I challenge you to make the Jabez prayer for blessing part of the daily fabric of your life. To do that, I encourage you to follow unwaveringly the plan outlined here for the next thirty days. By the end of that time, you'll be noticing significant changes in your life, and the prayer will be on its way to becoming a treasured, lifelong habit." The Amazon.com book description promises those "who commit to offering the same prayer on a regular basis will find themselves extravagantly blessed by God and enlarged agents of His miraculous power in everyday life."

Compare this to what Christ says about prayer:

Matthew 6: 7, 8

"When you pray, don't babble on and on as people of other religions do. They think their prayers
are answered merely by repeating their words again
and again. Don't be like them, for your Father
knows exactly what you need even before you ask
him!

The <u>Prayer of Jabez</u> sold nine million copies and was an international best-seller. By the time the craze was over, savvy marketers had created a Prayer of Jabez journal, devotional, bible study, a musical companion, key chains, mugs, backpacks, scented candles, and mouse pads.

The Lord honored Jabez and the prayer he uttered. It is in the bible. But followers of Christ might ask, did He include it in the bible so that people who live in the richest country in the world, obsessed with materialism, could petition Him daily to enrich them with more stuff?

Jesus displayed during His earthly ministry a command of the Old Testament and, as the Son of God most certainly was aware of Jabez. But when the disciples asked how to pray, instead of referring to Jabez, Jesus said:

Matthew 6: 9-18

Pray like this: Our Father in heaven, may your name be kept holy. May your Kingdom come soon. May your will be done on earth, as it is in heaven. Give us today the food we need, and forgive us our sins, as we have forgiven those who sin against us. And don't let us yield to temptation, but rescue us from the evil one.

If you forgive those who sin against you, your heavenly Father will forgive you. But if you refuse to forgive others, your Father will not forgive your sins.

And when you fast, don't make it obvious, as the hypocrites do, for they try to look miserable and disheveled so people will admire them for their fasting. I tell you the truth, that is the only reward they will ever get. But when you fast, comb your hair and wash your face. Then no one will notice that you are fasting, except your Father, who knows what you do in private. And your Father, who sees everything, will reward you.

Notice that Christ teaches us to ask for our daily sustenance, for forgiveness, and for strength against temptation. He goes on after describing how to pray by noting that the Father, who sees everything, will reward us.

The Jabez prayer, just like the tithe, is not a mechanical action that unfailingly results in another action, the automatic, robotic favor of God. Nor is the Lord a lottery that you have to play to win.

First seek the Lord. If the indwelling Spirit of God gives you a desire, He will also provide guidance on how to achieve it and what do with it once achieved. If your heart's desire comes from Him, he'll confirm it and provide the means to attain it in His time.

If there is something specific you want, ask the Lord to provide it. He knows what we need but He wants us to be in the habit of relying on Him, thus, there is every possibility He will provide something we want if we ask, and not, if we don't. Of paramount importance is where we keep the Lord. Do we want Him, or what He provides?

6 Poverty

Deuteronomy 15: 4-5

Save when there shall be no poor among you; for the LORD shall greatly bless thee in the land which the LORD thy God giveth thee for an inheritance to possess it: Only if thou carefully hearken unto the voice of the LORD thy God, to observe to do all these commandments which I command thee this day.

Deuteronomy 15: 11

For the poor shall never cease out of the land: therefore I command thee, saying, Thou shalt open thine hand wide unto thy brother, to thy poor, and to thy needy, in thy land.

7 Budgeting

Proverbs 6:6-8

Go to the ant, thou sluggard; consider her ways, and be wise:
Which having no guide, overseer, or ruler,
Provideth her meat in the summer, and gathereth her food in the harvest.

Proverbs 21:5

The thoughts of the diligent tend only to plenteousness; but of every one that is hasty only to want.

Proverbs 22:3

A prudent man foreseeth the evil, and hideth himself: but the simple pass on, and are punished.

Proverbs 24:3-4

Through wisdom is an house builded; and by understanding it is established: And by knowledge shall the chambers be filled with all precious and pleasant riches.

Proverbs 25:28

He that hath no rule over his own spirit is like a city that is broken down, and without walls.

Proverbs 27:23

Be thou diligent to know the state of thy flocks, and look well to thy herds.

Proverbs 27:26

The lambs are for thy clothing, and the goats are the price of the field.

Luke 14:28-30

For which of you, intending to build a tower, sitteth not down first, and counteth the cost, whether he have sufficient to finish it? Lest haply, after he hath laid the foundation, and is not able to finish it, all that behold it begin to mock him, Saying, This man began to build, and was not able to finish.

1 Corinthians 16:2

Upon the first day of the week let every one of you lay by him in store, as God hath prospered him, that there be no gatherings when I come.

8 Contentment

Psalm 23:1

The LORD is my shepherd, I shall not want.

Ecclesiastes 5:10

He that loveth silver shall not be satisfied with silver; nor he that loveth abundance with increase: this is also vanity.

Matthew 6:31-33

Therefore take no thought, saying, What shall we eat? or, What shall we drink? or, Wherewithal shall we be clothed? (For after all these things do the Gentiles seek:) for your heavenly Father knoweth that ye have need of all these things. **But seek ye first the kingdom of God, and his righteousness; and all these things shall be added unto you.**

Luke 3:14

And the soldiers likewise demanded of him, saying, And what shall we do? And he said unto them, Do violence to no man, neither accuse any falsely; and be content with your wages.

Philippians 4:11-13

Not that I speak in respect of want: for I have learned, in whatsoever state I am, therewith to be content. I know both how to be abased, and I know how to abound: every where and in all things I am instructed both to be full and to be hungry, both to abound and to suffer need. I can do all things through Christ which strengtheneth me.

1 Thessalonians 4:11

And that ye study to be quiet, and to do your own business, and to work with your own hands, as we commanded you...

1 Timothy 6:6

But godliness with contentment is great gain.

1 Timothy 6:7-10

For we brought nothing into this world, and it is certain we can carry nothing out. And having food and raiment let us be therewith content. But they that will be rich fall into temptation and a snare, and into many foolish and hurtful lusts, which drown men in destruction and perdition. For the love of money is the root of all evil: which while some coveted after, they have erred from the faith, and pierced themselves through with many sorrows.

Hebrews 13:5

Let your conversation be without covetousness; and be content with such things as ye have: for he hath said, I will never leave thee, nor forsake thee.

James 4:1-3

From whence come wars and fightings among you? come they not hence, even of your lusts that war in your members? Ye lust, and have not: ye kill, and desire to have, and cannot obtain: ye fight and war, yet ye have not, because ye ask not. Ye ask, and receive not, because ye ask amiss, that ye may consume it upon your lusts.

9 Debt

Exodus 22:14

And if a man borrow ought of his neighbour, and it be hurt, or die, the owner thereof being not with it, he shall surely make it good.

Deuteronomy 15:6

For the LORD thy God blesseth thee, as he promised thee: and thou shalt lend unto many nations, but thou shalt not borrow; and thou shalt reign over many nations, but they shall not reign over thee.

Deuteronomy 28:12

The LORD shall open unto thee his good treasure, the heaven to give the rain unto thy land in his season, and to bless all the work of thine hand: and thou shalt lend unto many nations, and thou shalt not borrow.

2 Kings 4:6-7

And it came to pass, when the vessels were full, that she said unto her son, Bring me yet a vessel. And he said unto her, There is not a vessel more. And the oil stayed. Then she came and told the man of God. And he said, Go, sell the oil, and pay thy debt, and live thou and thy children of the rest.

Psalm 37:21

The wicked borroweth, and payeth not again: but the righteous sheweth mercy, and giveth.

Proverbs 22:7

The rich ruleth over the poor, and the borrower is servant to the lender.

Proverbs 22:26-27

Be not thou one of them that strike hands, or of them that are sureties for debts. If thou hast nothing to pay, why should he take away thy bed from under thee?

Ecclesiastes 5:5

Better is it that thou shouldest not vow, than that thou shouldest vow and not pay.

Romans 13:8-10

Owe no man any thing, but to love one another: for he that loveth another hath fulfilled the law. For this, Thou shalt not commit adultery, Thou shalt not kill, Thou shalt not steal, Thou shalt not bear false witness, Thou shalt not covet; and if there be any other commandment, it is briefly comprehended in this saying, namely, Thou shalt love thy neighbour as thyself. Love worketh no ill to his neighbour: therefore love is the fulfilling of the law.

Commentary

L et's take a moment to think about what debt is, economically. If someone has excess capital that they aren't putting to use, they might make it available to someone else for a period of time.

They don't want to give up ownership of the asset, but they do want the asset to be productive, even though they aren't in a position to personally make it productive. You might have ten thousand dollars in an account, but you don't necessarily want to start a business with it. So the person who has saved capital makes an agreement with the other person who has a productive use for the capital. The borrower gets use of the money for a period of time, and agrees to repay the money, with interest, at negotiated times.

It certainly makes sense that of all the financial tools in our lives, we should want to limit how much interest we pay. Because we're losing not just the interest, but all the money we could have made if we had saved the interest.

That isn't good stewardship.

But what if our ability to be productive results from the loan itself?

Think of a corporation like Walmart. If Walmart wants to open a hundred new stores, they'll likely sell a few hundred million dollars worth of bonds. They'll use the proceeds of the bond sale to build the stores.

Then they'll repay the bonds and the interest out of the productivity they've created with the borrowed money. Because they know they're taking on a serious obligation, they crunch numbers until they're certain they will be able to not just repay the bonds and interest. They have to be able to create profit on top of that, or it isn't worth doing.

In the process, they're making products available and providing employment to thousands of people.

Does debt in that instance strike you as evil?

Of course not. But it is certainly not something that should be done lightly, without serious consideration. We need to think about whether what we're buying on credit is making us more productive, or whether it's making us less productive.

In this light, buying a television on credit is a bad idea, but taking out a student loan so you can get a better job someday and take better care of your family, that's not just defensible, it quite possibly demonstrates a lot of character and is a fine example of being a good steward of the capacity God put within you to be productive.

I find that the idea of debt is closely linked to—*but is secondary to*—the idea of stewardship. We are obligated to both work and be productive with the resources we've been given. Personally, I believe that being productive with money is just as important as being productive with any other resource that is in our care.

But like anything else, we need to approach it wisely, with eyes wide open, aware of the risks. The bible is clear about the risks.

> And if a man borrow ought of his neighbor, and it
> be hurt, or die, the owner thereof being not with it, he
> shall surely make it good. –Exodus 22: 14

A godly person who takes on debt takes on a solemn obligation to repay it. What's interesting to me about this verse isn't just that a person is obligated to repay the debt, but that in this example, if a person borrows something, say an animal, and the animal dies—or something happens that the borrower didn't anticipate, the borrower is still honor bound to make the other person whole.

Because debt is such a serious obligation, there's a great risk associated with being in debt.

> Just as the rich rule the poor, so the borrower is
> servant to the lender. –Proverbs 22: 7

Scriptures that deal with debt convey various meanings, none of which in context states that debt is evil. Exodus 22 tells us that if we borrow an item, we are responsible for the welfare of the item. Deuteronomy 15 and 28 tells us it is a blessing to be able to lend and not need to borrow. Psalm 37 says the wicked borrows and does not pay back—but the righteous gives. Ecclesiastes tells us it is better to not vow than vow and not pay.

In each case, debt is a morally neutral economic circumstance. It can't be a blessing to be able to lend money, if borrowing money is evil. That'd be like saying selling illegal drugs is a blessing, but buying them is a sin.

My personal belief is that the key to understanding the bible's take on debt is to frame it within the contexts of being productive and being a steward. Debt exists because it allows capital at rest to be put to work. That's good.

If you're going to create a debt, go into it aware that you're creating a solemn obligation, and make sure that you can repay that obligation without needing to resort to behavior that will displace God in your life.

10   Exploitation

Exodus 22: 22-25

Ye shall not afflict any widow, or fatherless child. If thou afflict them in any wise, and they cry at all unto me, I will surely hear their cry; And my wrath shall wax hot, and I will kill you with the sword; and your wives shall be widows, and your children fatherless. If thou lend money to any of my people that is poor by thee, thou shalt not be to him as an usurer, neither shalt thou lay upon him usury.

Leviticus 19:13

Thou shalt not defraud thy neighbour, neither rob him: the wages of him that is hired shall not abide with thee all night until the morning.

Deuteronomy 25:13-15

Thou shalt not have in thy bag divers weights, a great and a small. Thou shalt not have in thine house divers measures, a great and a small. But thou shalt have a perfect and just weight, a perfect and just measure shalt thou have: that thy days may be lengthened in the land which the LORD thy God giveth thee.

Job 31:13-14

If I did despise the cause of my manservant or of my maidservant, when they contended with me; What then shall I do when God riseth up? and when he visiteth, what shall I answer him?

Psalm 112:5

A good man sheweth favour, and lendeth: he will guide his affairs with discretion.

Proverbs 10:4

He becometh poor that dealeth with a slack hand: but the hand of the diligent maketh rich.

Proverbs 11:1

A false balance is abomination to the LORD: but a just weight is his delight.

Proverbs 13:4

The soul of the sluggard desireth, and hath nothing: but the soul of the diligent shall be made fat.

Proverbs 13:11

Wealth gotten by vanity shall be diminished: but he that gathereth by labour shall increase.

Proverbs 16:8

Better is a little with righteousness than great revenues without right.

Proverbs 22:16

He that oppresseth the poor to increase his riches, and he that giveth to the rich, shall surely come to want.

Jeremiah 22:13

Woe unto him that buildeth his house by unrighteousness, and his chambers by wrong; that useth his neighbour's service without wages, and giveth him not for his work...

Malachi 3:5

And I will come near to you to judgment; and I will be a swift witness against the sorcerers, and against the adulterers, and against false swearers, and against those that oppress the hireling in his wages, the widow, and the fatherless, and that turn aside the stranger from his right, and fear not me, saith the LORD of hosts.

Luke 16:10

He that is faithful in that which is least is faithful also in much: and he that is unjust in the least is unjust also in much.

Ephesians 6:9

And, ye masters, do the same things unto them, forbearing threatening: knowing that your Master also is in heaven; neither is there respect of persons with him.

Colossians 4:1

Masters, give unto your servants that which is just and equal; knowing that ye also have a Master in heaven.

1 Timothy 5:18

For the scripture saith, thou shalt not muzzle the ox that treadeth out the corn. And, The labourer is worthy of his reward.

James 5:4

Behold, the hire of the labourers who have reaped down your fields, which is of you kept back by fraud, crieth: and the cries of them which have reaped are entered into the ears of the Lord of sabaoth.

Commentary

> Woe to him who builds his house by unrighteousness, and his rooms by injustice; who uses his neighbor's service without wages, and doesn't give him his hire; who says, I will build me a wide house and spacious rooms, and cuts him out windows; and it is ceiling with cedar, and painted with vermilion.
>
> Shall you reign, because you strive to excel in cedar? Didn't your father eat and drink, and do justice and righteousness? Then it was well with him.
>
> He judged the cause of the poor and needy; then it was well. Wasn't this to know me? Says Yahweh.
>
> But your eyes and your heart are not but for your covetousness, and for shedding innocent blood, and for oppression, and for violence, to do it.
>
> Therefore thus says Yahweh concerning Jehoiakim the son of Josiah, king of Judah: they shall not lament for him, [saying], ah my brother! Or, Ah sister! They shall not lament for him, [saying] Ah lord! Or, ah his glory!
>
> He shall be buried with the burial of a donkey, drawn and cast forth beyond the gates of Jerusalem.
> --Jeremiah 22:13-19 (World English Bible)

Nobel laureate and bestselling author Daniel Kahneman, in *Thinking Fast and Slow*, cites a study that shows when human beings are subconsciously engaged to think about money, they are more likely to be tenacious in solving problems, and are less helpful to others—even if providing assistance could be done at little expense of time or energy.

We've all heard stories told by a gleeful person who bought an antique for a few hundred dollars from a widow who didn't realize it was worth thousands. A few years ago, a department store commercial played on the same theme. A woman emerges with her bags, walking quickly. She looks over her shoulder, and we learn the deals are so good, we'll feel like we're robbing the store. "Drive! Drive!" She shouts.

Our natures are programmed to fight for every dollar and when advantage occurs, seize it.

It's no wonder then that to some, a transaction is sweeter when a lopsided advantage is secured. One person sees another in a moment of weakness, or need, or ignorance, and sees an opportunity. "A fool is born every minute," he explains.

"You shall not mistreat any widow or fatherless child. If you do mistreat them, and they cry out to me, I will surely hear their cry, and my wrath will burn, and I will kill you with the sword, and your wives shall become widows and your children fatherless.

> "If you lend money to any of my people with you
> who is poor, you shall not be like a moneylender to
> him, and you shall not exact interest from him. If
> ever you take your neighbor's cloak in pledge, you
> shall return it to him before the sun goes down, for
> that is his only covering, and it is his cloak for his
> body; in what else shall he sleep? And if he cries to
> me, I will hear, for I am compassionate. --Exodus 22:
> 22-27

Similarly, in the business world, some feel contracts exist to enable the wiser, more nimble businessperson to lock in advantage, so that when his counterparty has a change of fortune, he remains bound to continue doing business at a disadvantage.

Contracts are necessary because they allow business partners to commit capital and know that their counterparts are likewise committed, and cannot abandon the deal. If you start a business with your brother-in-law and you agree to buy the first five thousand worth of goods, and he agrees to buy the second, a contract would protect you from the easily foreseeable risk of starting the business, hitting some bumpy roads, and your brother-in-law pulling out because he doesn't want to "throw good money after bad."

So while contracts are necessary to allow good stewards of money to protect their investments when they deploy resources, not all contracts exist to enforce mutually beneficial cooperation.

Imagine instead that your brother-in-law is an out-of-work genius mathematician with two Ph.Ds. from MIT. He has two weeks to come up with a mortgage payment or he loses his house. If that happens, your sister says, the marriage is over. Since he's financially dazed and reeling, you invite him to join your tech startup. He can't buy in as a partner, but you mine his genius, work him seventy hours a week, and pay him a third of what he could earn when the market for genius mathematicians returns. You earn ten million dollars and he makes a hundred thousand. You tell yourself that it's capitalism, that because you're the one taking the risk, you deserve the lion's share of the reward.

That's an entirely different kind of a contract—the business equivalent of finding an old lady who doesn't realize the '70 Mustang in the garage is worth more than a couple hundred dollars. Nothing changes in the work that the contract performs. In each case, two willing parties agree to be bound in the future to terms set today. Yet in the first contract, the aim is mutual profitability, and in the second, unbalanced profitability resulting from the exploitation of a man on his knees.

As Daniel Kahneman points out in Thinking, Fast and Slow, we become quite selfish when money enters our consciousness.

Whether arranging a long term contract or a single transaction, we quickly discern the stakes. If we can negotiate a better deal, we keep more of our money. We have more security and perhaps can take better care of our families.

Life creates imperatives. Life is hard. One day we get out of bed and our knees hurt. Or our backs twang like cords on a string bass, and we think, how long can I keep doing this? The more life we experience the more we understand that very little separates us from a world of violent change, tempestuous weather, life-ending cold in the winter and energy sapping heat in the summer. Political upheaval. Scams. Institutionalized injustice.

Sometimes it seems like the busiest, smartest people are working against us.

Sometimes it seems like just defending ourselves requires us to take advantage of others. Whether we negotiate a contract or haggle over a single transaction, we have to do the best we can.

The other guy? It's up to him to do the same.

Yet.

Where is the line between being a good steward, understanding the value of our money and not parting with it foolishly, and making another human being the object of exploitation?

It's a matter of place and context, whether we see ourselves as alone, eating or being eaten in a Darwinian forest of scarce resources, versus seeing ourselves as part of a two-part hierarchy, God above, and us below, shoulder to shoulder with seven billion others.

> Masters, provide your slaves with what is right and fair, because you know that you also have a Master in heaven. --Colossians 4:1

Just as climbing a ladder might get you ten feet closer to the sun but doesn't increase the warmth on your face, we are no closer to God by being a master over a servant, or by perceiving ourselves superior to the man or woman beside us. The distance between God above and us below is humbling. Examining it we are impressed by how common is our plight with our fellow human beings. No matter how superior I feel to another man, I am infinitely inferior to the Almighty above, and in that, I am a brother to the lowest man on earth. I am no better than anyone, and thus, everyone deserves my best.

But the man who never feels tiny compared to the Almighty is persuaded that the distance between him and the man he swindles is great. He is unable to put his inner animal in check, and to realize that his highest pursuit isn't temporal—survival, money and wealth—but is instead eternal—the rewards that arise from sculpting one's life to resemble the LORD as much as possible. And so the animal man tears into his fellow like a lion into a gazelle. He tells himself that if the swindled man was more responsible, he wouldn't be getting swindled. It's almost a kindness to take his money because doing so will wake him up to the fact that the world is a tough place. The next time he won't be such an easy victim.

Only by ignoring God are we able to pretend one of us is better than another, or that another is a fitting object of exploitation.

So how are we to behave?

> The Lord detests dishonest scales, but accurate
> weights find favor with him. --Proverbs 11:1

The LORD delights in a just weight because a just weight doesn't change when the other party to a transaction is feeble, uninformed, desperate, or of a different color or sex or intelligence. A just weight is just for the rich and the poor, the warm and the cold, the fed and the hungry. A just weight stands like God, true, regardless of changing circumstances, perceptions, or desires.

We are not called to find weakness in others and exploit it.

We are called to love one another, and this suggests a simple way to think about business and exploitation. To gain clarity, think of your business deals this way:

Does the person you are working with stand to benefit from the transaction as much as you? Then be a good steward and be diligent in making a fair transaction. Respect the resources God gave you and retain their full value when you trade them. If the deal is good, and your counterparty is also a good steward, all will walk away from the deal feeling richer. In a free society composed of virtuous people, that's how capitalism is supposed to work.

For we are his workmanship, created in Christ Jesus for good works, which God prepared before that we would walk in them. –Ephesians 2:10

On the other hand, if you're dealing with a person whose disadvantage compels him to act for a short term gain that is against his long term benefit, whether he understands it or not, instead of seeking a trade, perhaps the good work that God has prepared for you to walk in is to pull the disadvantaged man back to his feet, and then advance together into mutual profitability.

11 Getting Rich Quickly

Exodus 23:12

Six days thou shalt do thy work, and on the seventh day thou shalt rest: that thine ox and thine ass may rest, and the son of thy handmaid, and the stranger, may be refreshed.

Proverbs 28:19-20

He that tilleth his land shall have plenty of bread: but he that followeth after vain persons shall have poverty enough. A faithful man shall abound with blessings: but he that maketh haste to be rich shall not be innocent.

Proverbs 12:11

He that tilleth his land shall be satisfied with bread: but he that followeth vain persons is void of understanding.

Proverbs 13:11

Wealth gotten by vanity shall be diminished: but he that gathereth by labour shall increase.

Proverbs 14:15

The simple believeth every word: but the prudent man looketh well to his going.

Proverbs 19:2

Also, that the soul be without knowledge, it is not good; and he that hasteth with his feet sinneth.

Proverbs 21:5

The thoughts of the diligent tend only to plenteousness; but of every one that is hasty only to want.

Proverbs 23:4

Labour not to be rich: cease from thine own wisdom.

12 Giving

Deuteronomy 15:10

Thou shalt surely give him, and thine heart shall not be grieved when thou givest unto him: because that for this thing the LORD thy God shall bless thee in all thy works, and in all that thou puttest thine hand unto.

Deuteronomy 16:17

Every man shall give as he is able, according to the blessing of the LORD thy God which he hath given thee.

1 Chronicles 29:9

Then the people rejoiced, for that they offered willingly, because with perfect heart they offered willingly to the LORD: and David the king also rejoiced with great joy.

Proverbs 3:9-10

Honour the LORD with thy substance, and with the firstfruits of all thine increase: So shall thy barns be filled with plenty, and thy presses shall burst out with new wine.

Malachi 3:10

Bring ye all the tithes into the storehouse, that there may be meat in mine house, and prove me now herewith, saith the LORD of hosts, if I will not open you the windows of heaven, and pour you out a blessing, that there shall not be room enough to receive it.

Proverbs 3:27

Withhold not good from them to whom it is due, when it is in the power of thine hand to do it.

Proverbs 11:24-25

There is that scattereth, and yet increaseth; and there is that withholdeth more than is meet, but it tendeth to poverty. The liberal soul shall be made fat: and he that watereth shall be watered also himself.

Proverbs 21:26

He coveteth greedily all the day long: but the righteous giveth and spareth not.

Proverbs 22:9

He that hath a bountiful eye shall be blessed; for he giveth of his bread to the poor.

Luke 3:11

He answereth and saith unto them, He that hath two coats, let him impart to him that hath none; and he that hath meat, let him do likewise.

Luke 6:30

Give to every man that asketh of thee; and of him that taketh away thy goods ask them not again.

Proverbs 28:27

He that giveth unto the poor shall not lack: but he that hideth his eyes shall have many a curse.

Matthew 6:3-4

But when thou doest alms, let not thy left hand know what thy right hand doeth: That thine alms may be in secret: and thy Father which seeth in secret himself shall reward thee openly

Mark 12: 41-44

And Jesus sat over against the treasury, and beheld how the people cast money into the treasury: and many that were rich cast in much. And there came a certain poor widow, and she threw in two mites, which make a farthing. And he called unto him his disciples, and saith unto them, Verily I say unto you, That this poor widow hath cast more in, than all they which have cast into the treasury: For all they did cast in of their abundance; but she of her want did cast in all that she had, even all her living.

Luke 6:38

Give, and it shall be given unto you; good measure, pressed down, and shaken together, and running over, shall men give into your bosom. For with the same measure that ye mete withal it shall be measured to you again.

Acts 20:35

I have shewed you all things, how that so labouring ye ought to support the weak, and to remember the words of the Lord Jesus, how he said, It is more blessed to give than to receive.

Romans 12:8

Or he that exhorteth, on exhortation: he that giveth, let him do it with simplicity; he that ruleth, with diligence; he that sheweth mercy, with cheerfulness.

2 Corinthians 9:6-8

But this I say, He which soweth sparingly shall reap also sparingly; and he which soweth bountifully shall reap also bountifully. Every man according as he purposeth in his heart, so let him give; not grudgingly, or of necessity: for God loveth a cheerful giver. And God is able to make all grace abound toward you; that ye, always having all sufficiency in all things, may abound to every good work...

2 Corinthians 9:10

Now he that ministereth seed to the sower both minister bread for your food, and multiply your seed sown, and increase the fruits of your righteousness...

Galatians 6:7

Be not deceived; God is not mocked: for whatsoever a man soweth, that shall he also reap.

Philippians 4:15-17

Now ye Philippians know also, that in the beginning of the gospel, when I departed from Macedonia, no church communicated with me as concerning giving and receiving, but ye only. For even in Thessalonica ye sent once and again unto my necessity. Not because I desire a gift: but I desire fruit that may abound to your account.

James 2:15-16

If a brother or sister be naked, and destitute of daily food, And one of you say unto them, Depart in peace, be ye warmed and filled; notwithstanding ye give them not those things which are needful to the body; what doth it profit?

13 Investing

Proverbs 15:22

Without counsel purposes are disappointed: but in the multitude of counsellors they are established.

Proverbs 24:27

Prepare thy work without, and make it fit for thyself in the field; and afterwards build thine house.

Proverbs 28:20

A faithful man shall abound with blessings: but he that maketh haste to be rich shall not be innocent.

Proverbs 13:11

Wealth gotten by vanity shall be diminished: but he that gathereth by labour shall increase.

Proverbs 19:2

Also, that the soul be without knowledge, it is not good; and he that hasteth with his feet sinneth.

Ecclesiastes 11:2

Give a portion to seven, and also to eight; for thou knowest not what evil shall be upon the earth.

Matthew 25:14-30

For the kingdom of heaven is as a man travelling into a far country, who called his own servants, and delivered unto them his goods. And unto one he gave five talents, to another two, and to another one; to every man according to his several ability; and straightway took his journey. Then he that had received the five talents went and traded with the same, and made them other five talents. And likewise he that had received two, he also gained other two. But he that had received one went and digged in the earth, and hid his lord's money. After a long time the lord of those servants cometh, and reckoneth with them. And so he that had received five talents came and brought other five talents, saying, Lord, thou deliveredst unto me five talents: behold, I have gained beside them five talents more. His lord said unto him, Well done, thou good and faithful servant: thou hast been faithful over a few things, I will make thee ruler over many things: enter thou into the joy of thy lord. He also that had received two talents came and said, Lord, thou deliveredst unto me two talents: behold, I have gained two other talents beside them. His lord said unto him, Well done, good and faithful servant; thou hast been faithful over a few things, I will make thee ruler over many things: enter thou into the joy of thy lord. Then he which had received the one talent came and said, Lord, I knew thee that thou art an hard man, reaping where thou hast not sown, and gathering where thou hast not strawed: And I was afraid, and went and hid thy talent in the earth: lo, there thou hast that is thine. His lord answered and said unto him, Thou wicked and slothful servant, thou knewest that I reap where I sowed not, and gather where I have not strawed: Thou oughtest therefore to have put my money to the exchangers, and then at my coming I should have received mine own with usury. Take therefore the talent from him, and give it unto him which hath ten talents. For unto every one that hath shall be given, and he shall have abundance: but from him that hath not shall be taken away even that which he hath. And cast ye the unprofitable servant into outer dark-ness: there shall be weeping and gnashing of teeth.

Commentary

I nvesting is tied to saving. Saving is setting aside money so that it accumulates. Investing is putting it to use so that it both accomplishes something and becomes more valuable as it does so. That's a very key distinction to be aware of.

Whereas saving assumes we're looking for safety, so the money is there in the future, investing assumes risk, as when we put money to use there's never any guarantee that it'll actually accomplish what we want it to.

Remember the example of the Walmart bonds, for instance. Walmart borrows capital by issuing bonds, puts the money to use building stores, and then accomplishes good by employing people and providing products that consumers want.

In this sense, Walmart's use of the money is an investment. Just as the people who bought Walmart bonds were investing. They get a return on the money, it grows, and the money does work that is meaningful.

At the same time, though, there's no guarantee that after Walmart builds a store, that people will actually shop there. So if we're going to invest money so that it achieves things, let's look at what the Bible says about investing, starting with Proverbs 15: 22.

> Without counsel purposes are disappointed: but in
> the multitude of counselors they are established.

First, broadly speaking, when you have "purposes" you want to achieve, you should avail yourself of counsellors, or people who can provide new insights for you. That's how you can achieve your purposes.

> Prepare thy work without, and make it fit for thy-
> self in the field; and afterwards build thine house.
> –Proverbs 24: 27

This one sounds like a riddle at first by yields a lot of common sense: don't build a house before you have a means of supporting yourself. Get the field going first. Invest in your capacity to be productive before you take on obligations based on your expected productivity.

Or, don't buy a nice car the day you start college. Wait until you get a job.

Investing isn't just about putting money at risk in the stock market in the hope of getting a return. Investing is also tied to stewardship and work. Investing means you're taking a resource and cultivating it so it becomes something more than it was. Whether that's turning a pile of dollars into a bigger pile, or turning a skill for math into a degree in math, and then a job as a mathematician.

This verse speaks to me because it's really saying, to get along in this world you have to be productive, you have to make things happen before you can enjoy the fruits of productivity.

Proverbs 28: 20 supports this premise.

> A faithful man shall abound with blessings: but he
> that maketh haste to be rich shall not be innocent.

What is a faithful person? Is it someone who just believes in God? Or someone who acts on that faith and lives according to the rules that God has established?

I don't think that this is saying that because a person merely believes that God exists, God rewards him.

Here a faithful man is the one who is living right. He's keeping God first, working hard, saving, investing and creating value, taking care of his family, exercising prudence, and because of it, is experiencing blessings.

I think the point is that faithful living actually, over time, creates the blessings.

Meaning that if you do the right things, the world is ordered by God so that you have a bountiful life. Whereas the person who takes shortcuts, the person who puts money before God, can't help but to run afoul of the rules, and can't help but to sin.

Whereas the person in Proverbs 28: 20, who takes shortcuts and puts money before God, can't help but to run afoul of the rules, and can't help but to sin:

> A faithful man shall abound with blessings: but *he that maketh haste to be rich shall not be innocent.*

Ecclesiastes 11: 2 is the most quoted verse regarding investing that I've seen.

> Give a portion to seven, and also to eight; for thou knowest not what evil shall be upon the earth.

"Give a portion to seven" means spread around your resources in multiple places, because you don't know what's going to happen in the future. This is the oldest way there is of saying, don't put all of your eggs in one basket.

In investing, of course, this means diversify your assets. Invest a little in this area, and a little in that area.

The deeper lesson is to be mindful of risks. I think the most fundamental understanding we can take here is that in dealing with our money, we need to value it enough to be aware of risks and take action to mitigate them.

The lesson is not to avoid risk altogether, because if it was, the verse would have said, "bury your money in a jar."

The fact is that in order for money to be productive, it has to be at risk, to some degree or another. God wants us to be productive with our money, but to contemplate the risks, and take appropriate steps to ensure that if we suffer a loss, it will be comparatively small.

14 Lending

Exodus 22:25

If thou lend money to any of my people that is poor by thee, thou shalt not be to him as an usurer, neither shalt thou lay upon him usury.

Leviticus 25:35-37

And if thy brother be waxen poor, and fallen in decay with thee; then thou shalt relieve him: yea, though he be a stranger, or a sojourner; that he may live with thee. Take thou no usury of him, or increase: but fear thy God; that thy brother may live with thee. Thou shalt not give him thy money upon usury, nor lend him thy victuals for increase.

Psalm 37:26

He is ever merciful, and lendeth; and his seed is blessed.

Deuteronomy 15:8

But thou shalt open thine hand wide unto him, and shalt surely lend him sufficient for his need, in that which he wanteth.

Deuteronomy 23:19-20

Thou shalt not lend upon usury to thy brother; usury of money, usury of victuals, usury of any thing that is lent upon usury: Unto a stranger thou mayest lend upon usury; but unto thy brother thou shalt not lend upon usury: that the LORD thy God may bless thee in all that thou settest thine hand to in the land whither thou goest to possess it.

Deuteronomy 24:10

When thou dost lend thy brother any thing, thou shalt not go into his house to fetch his pledge.

Proverbs 3:27-28

Withhold not good from them to whom it is due, when it is in the power of thine hand to do it. Say not unto thy neighbour, Go, and come again, and to morrow I will give; when thou hast it by thee.

Nehemiah 5: 1-13

And there was a great cry of the people and of their wives against their brethren the Jews. For there were that said, We, our sons, and our daughters, are many: therefore we take up corn for them, that we may eat, and live. Some also there were that said, We have mortgaged our lands, vineyards, and houses, that we might buy corn, because of the dearth. There were also that said, We have borrowed money for the king's tribute, and that upon our lands and vineyards. Yet now our flesh is as the flesh of our brethren, our children as their children:

and, lo, we bring into bondage our sons and our daughters to be servants, and some of our daughters are brought unto bondage already: neither is it in our power to redeem them; for other men have our lands and vineyards. And I was very angry when I heard their cry and these words. Then I consulted with myself, and I rebuked the nobles, and the rulers, and said unto them, Ye exact usury, every one of his brother. And I set a great assembly against them. And I said unto them, We after our ability have redeemed our brethren the Jews, which were sold unto the heathen; and will ye even sell your brethren? or shall they be sold unto us? Then held they their peace, and found nothing to answer. Also I said, It is not good that ye do: ought ye not to walk in the fear of our God because of the reproach of the heathen our enemies? I likewise, and my brethren, and my servants, might exact of them money and corn: I pray you, let us leave off this usury. Restore, I pray you, to them, even this day, their lands, their vineyards, their oliveyards, and their houses, also the hundredth part of the money, and of the corn, the wine, and the oil, that ye exact of them. Then said they, We will restore them, and will require nothing of them; so will we do as thou sayest. Then I called the priests, and took an oath of them, that they should do according to this promise. Also I shook my lap, and said, So God shake out every man from his house, and from his labour, that performeth not this promise, even thus be he shaken out, and emptied. And all the congregation said, Amen, and praised the LORD. And the people did according to this promise.

Psalm 15:5

He that putteth not out his money to usury, nor taketh reward against the innocent. He that doeth these things shall never be moved.

Psalm 112:5

A good man sheweth favour, and lendeth: he will guide his affairs with discretion.

Proverbs 28:8

He that by usury and unjust gain increaseth his substance, he shall gather it for him that will pity the poor.

Matthew 5:42

Give to him that asketh thee, and from him that would borrow of thee turn not thou away.

Luke 6:35

But love ye your enemies, and do good, and lend, hoping for nothing again; and your reward shall be great, and ye shall be the children of the Highest: for he is kind unto the unthankful and to the evil.

15   Legacy

Matthew 6:20-21

But lay up for yourselves treasures in heaven, where neither moth nor rust doth corrupt, and where thieves do not break through nor steal: For where your treasure is, there will your heart be also.

2 Timothy 2:2

And the things that thou hast heard of me among many witnesses, the same commit thou to faithful men, who shall be able to teach others also.

Deuteronomy 6:5-7

And thou shalt love the Lord thy God with all thine heart, and with all thy soul, and with all thy might. And these words, which I command thee this day, shall be in thine heart: And thou shalt teach them diligently unto thy children, and shalt talk of them when thou sittest in thine house, and when thou walkest by the way, and when thou liest down, and when thou risest up.

Proverbs 13:22

A good man leaveth an inheritance to his children's children: and the wealth of the sinner is laid up for the just.

16 Love of Money

Matthew 19:21-26

Jesus said unto him, If thou wilt be perfect, go and sell that thou hast, and give to the poor, and thou shalt have treasure in heaven: and come and follow me. But when the young man heard that saying, he went away sorrowful: for he had great possessions. Then said Jesus unto his disciples, Verily I say unto you, That a rich man shall hardly enter into the kingdom of heaven. And again I say unto you, It is easier for a camel to go through the eye of a needle, than for a rich man to enter into the kingdom of God. When his disciples heard it, they were exceedingly amazed, saying, Who then can be saved? But Jesus beheld them, and said unto them, With men this is impossible; but with God all things are possible.

Mark 4:19

And the cares of this world, and the deceitfulness of riches, and the lusts of other things entering in, choke the word, and it becometh unfruitful.

James 5:1-6

Go to now, ye rich men, weep and howl for your miseries that shall come upon you. Your riches are corrupted, and your garments are motheaten. Your gold and silver is cankered; and the rust of them shall be a witness against you, and shall eat your flesh as it were fire. Ye have heaped treasure together for the last days. Behold, the hire of the labourers who have reaped down your fields, which is of you kept back by fraud, crieth: and the cries of them which have reaped are entered into the ears of the Lord of sabaoth. Ye have lived in pleasure on the earth, and been wanton; ye have nourished your hearts, as in a day of slaughter. Ye have condemned and killed the just; and he doth not resist you.

17 Planning

Genesis 41:34-36

Let Pharaoh do this, and let him appoint officers over the land, and take up the fifth part of the land of Egypt in the seven plenteous years. And let them gather all the food of those good years that come, and lay up corn under the hand of Pharaoh, and let them keep food in the cities. And that food shall be for store to the land against the seven years of famine, which shall be in the land of Egypt; that the land perish not through the famine.

Proverbs 6:6-8

Go to the ant, thou sluggard; consider her ways, and be wise: Which having no guide, overseer, or ruler, Provideth her meat in the summer, and gathereth her food in the harvest.

Proverbs 13:16

Every prudent man dealeth with knowledge: but a fool layeth open his folly.

Proverbs 13:19

The desire accomplished is sweet to the soul: but it is abomination to fools to depart from evil.

Proverbs 16:1

The preparations of the heart in man, and the answer of the tongue, is from the LORD.

Proverbs 16:9

A man's heart deviseth his way: but the LORD directeth his steps.

Proverbs 20:18

Every purpose is established by counsel: and with good advice make war.

Proverbs 21:5

The thoughts of the diligent tend only to plenteousness; but of every one that is hasty only to want.

Proverbs 22:3

A prudent man foreseeth the evil, and hideth himself: but the simple pass on, and are punished.

Proverbs 24:3-4

Through wisdom is an house builded; and by understanding it is established: And by knowledge shall the chambers be filled with all precious and pleasant riches.

Proverbs 24:27

Prepare thy work without, and make it fit for thyself in the field; and afterwards build thine house.

Proverbs 27:12

A prudent man foreseeth the evil, and hideth himself; but the simple pass on, and are punished.

Proverbs 27:23

Be thou diligent to know the state of thy flocks, and look well to thy herds.

Ecclesiastes 11:2

Give a portion to seven, and also to eight; for thou knowest not what evil shall be upon the earth.

Matthew 25:1-13

Then shall the kingdom of heaven be likened unto ten virgins, which took their lamps, and went forth to meet the bridegroom. And five of them were wise, and five were foolish. They that were foolish took their lamps, and took no oil with them: But the wise took oil in their vessels with their lamps. While the bridegroom tarried, they all slumbered and slept. And at midnight there was a cry made, Behold, the bridegroom cometh; go ye out to meet him. Then all those virgins arose, and trimmed their lamps. And the foolish said unto the wise, Give us of your oil; for our lamps are gone out. But the wise answered, saying, Not so; lest there be not enough for us and you: but go ye rather to them that sell, and buy for yourselves. And while they went to buy, the bridegroom came; and they that were ready went in with him to the marriage: and the door was shut. Afterward came also the other virgins, saying, Lord, Lord, open to us. But he answered and said, Verily I say unto you, I know you not. Watch therefore, for ye know neither the day nor the hour wherein the Son of man cometh.

Luke 12:16-21

And he spake a parable unto them, saying, The ground of a certain rich man brought forth plentifully: And he thought within himself, saying, What shall I do, because I have no room where to bestow my fruits? And he said, This will I do: I will pull down my barns, and build greater; and there will I bestow all my fruits and my goods. And I will say to my soul, Soul, thou hast much goods laid up for many years; take thine ease, eat, drink, and be merry. But God said unto him, Thou fool, this night thy soul shall be required of thee: then whose shall those things be, which thou hast provided? So is he that layeth up treasure for himself, and is not rich toward God.

Luke 14:28-30

For which of you, intending to build a tower, sitteth not down first, and counteth the cost, whether he have sufficient to finish it? Lest haply, after he hath laid the foundation, and is not able to finish it, all that behold it begin to mock him, Saying, This man began to build, and was not able to finish.

1 Corinthians 16:1-2

Now concerning the collection for the saints, as I have given order to the churches of Galatia, even so do ye. Upon the first day of the week let every one of you lay by him in store, as God hath prospered him, that there be no gatherings when I come.

1 Timothy 6:7

For we brought nothing into this world, and it is certain we can carry nothing out.

18 Provision

Nehemiah 6:9

For they all made us afraid, saying, Their hands shall be weakened from the work, that it be not done. Now therefore, O God, strengthen my hands.

1 Kings 17:13-16

And Elijah said unto her, Fear not; go and do as thou hast said: but make me thereof a little cake first, and bring it unto me, and after make for thee and for thy son. For thus saith the LORD God of Israel, The barrel of meal shall not waste, neither shall the cruse of oil fail, until the day that the LORD sendeth rain upon the earth. And she went and did according to the saying of Elijah: and she, and he, and her house, did eat many days. And the barrel of meal wasted not, neither did the cruse of oil fail, according to the word of the LORD, which he spake by Elijah.

Psalm 37:25

I have been young, and now am old; yet have I not seen the righteous forsaken, nor his seed begging bread.

Matthew 6:31-32

Therefore take no thought, saying, What shall we eat? or, What shall we drink? or, Wherewithal shall we be clothed? (For after all these things do the Gentiles seek:) for your heavenly Father knoweth that ye have need of all these things.

Matthew 7:11

If ye then, being evil, know how to give good gifts unto your children, how much more shall your Father which is in heaven give good things to them that ask him?

Luke 12:7

But even the very hairs of your head are all numbered. Fear not therefore: ye are of more value than many sparrows.

John 21:6

And he said unto them, Cast the net on the right side of the ship, and ye shall find. They cast therefore, and now they were not able to draw it for the multitude of fishes.

2 Corinthians 9:8-15

And God is able to make all grace abound toward you; that ye, always having all sufficiency in all things, may abound to every good work: (As it is written,

He hath dispersed abroad; he hath given to the poor: his righteousness remaineth for ever. Now he that ministereth seed to the sower both minister bread for your food, and multiply your seed sown, and increase the fruits of your righteousness;) Being enriched in every thing to all bountifulness, which causeth through us thanksgiving to God. For the administration of this service not only supplieth the want of the saints, but is abundant also by many thanksgivings unto God; Whiles by the experiment of this ministration they glorify God for your professed subjection unto the gospel of Christ, and for your liberal distribution unto them, and unto all men; And by their prayer for you, which long after you for the exceeding grace of God in you. Thanks be unto God for his unspeakable gift.

Philippians 4:19

But my God shall supply all your need according to his riches in glory by Christ Jesus.

19   Prospering

Genesis 26:12

Then Isaac sowed in that land, and received in the same year an hundredfold: and the LORD blessed him.

Genesis 39:3

And his master saw that the LORD was with him, and that the LORD made all that he did to prosper in his hand.

Deuteronomy 24:19

When thou cuttest down thine harvest in thy field, and hast forgot a sheaf in the field, thou shalt not go again to fetch it: it shall be for the stranger, for the fatherless, and for the widow: that the LORD thy God may bless thee in all the work of thine hands.

Deuteronomy 8:18

But thou shalt remember the LORD thy God: for it is he that giveth thee power to get wealth, that he may establish his covenant which he sware unto thy fathers, as it is this day.

Deuteronomy 15:10

Thou shalt surely give him, and thine heart shall not be grieved when thou givest unto him: because that for this thing the LORD thy God shall bless thee in all thy works, and in all that thou puttest thine hand unto.

Deuteronomy 30:8-10

And thou shalt return and obey the voice of the LORD, and do all his commandments which I command thee this day. And the LORD thy God will make thee plenteous in every work of thine hand, in the fruit of thy body, and in the fruit of thy cattle, and in the fruit of thy land, for good: for the LORD will again rejoice over thee for good, as he rejoiced over thy fathers: If thou shalt hearken unto the voice of the LORD thy God, to keep his commandments and his statutes which are written in this book of the law, and if thou turn unto the LORD thy God with all thine heart, and with all thy soul.

1 Corinthians 16:2

Upon the first day of the week let every one of you lay by him in store, as God hath prospered him, that there be no gatherings when I come.

Joshua 1:8

This book of the law shall not depart out of thy mouth; but thou shalt meditate therein day and night, that thou mayest observe to do according to all that is written therein: for then thou shalt make thy way prosperous, and then thou shalt have good success.

1 Chronicles 22:12

Only the LORD give thee wisdom and understanding, and give thee charge concerning Israel, that thou mayest keep the law of the LORD thy God.

2 Chronicles 31:20-21

And thus did Hezekiah throughout all Judah, and wrought that which was good and right and truth before the LORD his God. And in every work that he began in the service of the house of God, and in the law, and in the commandments, to seek his God, he did it with all his heart, and prospered.

Jeremiah 17:8

For he shall be as a tree planted by the waters, and that spreadeth out her roots by the river, and shall not see when heat cometh, but her leaf shall be green; and shall not be careful in the year of drought, neither shall cease from yielding fruit.

Psalm 1: 1-3

Blessed is the man that walketh not in the counsel of the ungodly, nor standeth in the way of sinners, nor sitteth in the seat of the scornful. But his delight is in the law of the LORD; and in his law doth he meditate day and night. And he shall be like a tree planted by the rivers of water, that bringeth forth his fruit in his season; his leaf also shall not wither; and whatsoever he doeth shall prosper.

Psalm 35:27

Let them shout for joy, and be glad, that favour my righteous cause: yea, let them say continually, Let the LORD be magnified, which hath pleasure in the prosperity of his servant.

Malachi 3:10

Bring ye all the tithes into the storehouse, that there may be meat in mine house, and prove me now herewith, saith the LORD of hosts, if I will not open you the windows of heaven, and pour you out a blessing, that there shall not be room enough to receive it.

3 John 1:2

Beloved, I wish above all things that thou mayest prosper and be in health, even as thy soul prospereth.

20   Receiving

Ecclesiastes 5:19

Every man also to whom God hath given riches and wealth, and hath given him power to eat thereof, and to take his portion, and to rejoice in his labour; this is the gift of God.

Acts 20:35

I have shewed you all things, how that so labouring ye ought to support the weak, and to remember the words of the Lord Jesus, how he said, It is more blessed to give than to receive.

1 Corinthians 9:10-11

Or saith he it altogether for our sakes? For our sakes, no doubt, this is written: that he that ploweth should plow in hope; and that he that thresheth in hope should be partaker of his hope. If we have sown unto you spiritual things, is it a great thing if we shall reap your carnal things?

John 3:27

John answered and said, A man can receive nothing, except it be given him from heaven.

1 Timothy 5:18

For the scripture saith, thou shalt not muzzle the ox that treadeth out the corn. And, The labourer is worthy of his reward.

21 Saving

Genesis 41: 47-49; 53-54

And in the seven plenteous years the earth brought forth by handfuls.

And he gathered up all the food of the seven years, which were in the land of Egypt, and laid up the food in the cities: the food of the field, which was round about every city, laid he up in the same.

And Joseph gathered corn as the sand of the sea, very much, until he left numbering; for it was without number.

And the seven years of plenteousness, that was in the land of Egypt, were ended.

And the seven years of dearth began to come, according as Joseph had said: and the dearth was in all lands; but in all the land of Egypt there was bread.

Proverbs 21:5

The thoughts of the diligent tend only to plenteousness; but of every one that is hasty only to want.

Proverbs 21:20

There is treasure to be desired and oil in the dwelling of the wise; but a foolish man spendeth it up.

Proverbs 30:24-29

There be four things which are little upon the earth, but they are exceeding wise: The ants are a people not strong, yet they prepare their meat in the summer; The conies are but a feeble folk, yet make they their houses in the rocks; The locusts have no king, yet go they forth all of them by bands; The spider taketh hold with her hands, and is in kings' palaces.

Proverbs 27:12

A prudent man foreseeth the evil, and hideth himself; but the simple pass on, and are punished.

1 Corinthians 16:2

Upon the first day of the week let every one of you lay by him in store, as God hath prospered him, that there be no gatherings when I come.

Commentary

We've all heard so many rules about saving that it's easy to lose sight of why the rules of thumb about saving money exist. I always heard growing up that we're supposed to save 10 percent of our income. The financial planning system I use prefers 15 percent. A scholar I admire recently wrote that some people need to save 30 to 40 percent of their incomes. After taxes, I don't know what they're supposed to buy groceries with.

The clearest verses that deal with saving are in Genesis. Joseph dreams there will be seven years of plenty, so he gathers up food during those seven years and sets it aside. Then when the seven years of plenty are passed, "in all of Egypt there is bread."

Notice that the verse doesn't say that Joseph saved a certain percentage. It says he saved a lot—"he gathered corn as the sand of the sea, very much... without number."

> The prudent man foresees the evil and hides from it. —Proverbs 27: 12

There is no right per cent to save. In modern financial planning we like to use rules of thumb like saving 15 percent, but what's really going on in the Bible when they're saving is that they're anticipating future needs, and saving appropriately.

Also, Proverbs 13:11 says

> Dishonest money dwindles away, but he who gathers money little by little makes it grow.

That sure sounds like we ought to make a habit of saving money.

It's interesting that Luke says it makes sense that if you're going to build a tower, that you should make some calculations regarding your resources.

> For which of you, intending to build a tower,
> sitteth not down first, and counteth the cost, whether
> he have sufficient to finish it? --Luke 14: 28

To me, the lack of any specific rule for how much to save, but the repeated advice to do so, combined with what we know about work, debt and stewardship, leads me to a single place.

We are to look forward, we're to save so that we avoid hardship, and we're to make our money productive as well. The point of saving is not to get rich and become idle. It's to avoid hardship, continue to be productive, and expand our economic capacity to do God's work.

What follows is a more technical look at saving.

A common question: "Why should I suspend my 401(k) contribution to build savings, especially when I'm getting a higher return, a fifty percent match, and I have a 401k loan provision?"

Financial health is not commonly possible without savings that are safe, liquid, and accessible without permission, penalty, or fee. In a personal economy, savings form a foundation that makes great efficiencies possible. Savings makes prosperity possible.

According to FRED (Federal Reserve Economic Data), the average <u>American saves 5.7</u>% of income and <u>pays 9.9% to debt service</u>. Both have improved since 2008. For too many Americans, debt interest siphons money that would be more beneficially directed toward building a foundation of savings. Instead, households are often built on debt.

Although financial advisors often advise their clients to keep six months' income in a "rainy day" fund, for a variety of reasons, most Americans don't. We pay others first, ourselves last, and consume what we want. We believe we have plenty of time to make difficult financial decisions—especially those we perceive will limit immediate enjoyment of our resources. Finally, savings dollars are considered low-return money, which, in pursuit of efficiency, should be limited. Thus we allocate money to speculative assets because savings accounts offer low yields.

Internal Rate of Return

It is not possible to argue that the growth potential of a savings account surpasses that of an equity account. The yield on a savings account, however, is not its prime attraction. Safety and liquidity are primary because they ensure that financial surprises don't derail an entire life's economic potential. The first use of savings in a financial plan is as an extension of the financial vehicles we purchase that protect us from economic loss—covering deductibles and other short term or emergency liquidity needs.

Investing—putting money at risk, and saving—storing money in a safe place, are very different. Saving in a 401(k) is a non sequitur. A defense with a fifty percent fail rate is not a defense, it is further risk.

Although monies might earn a greater return in risk assets than a savings account, it is impossible to guarantee that they will earn more than could be lost by failing to have liquid funds when hardship or disaster strikes. Even if liquidity has a terrible return, prudence demands it remain a core element in every financial plan. However, viewing savings as exclusively defensive predisposes us to the mindset that savings is a "necessary evil." We fret that money in our savings account isn't working as hard as it could be.

This is problematic because by limiting savings, we cut short other benefits that derive from having access to liquid and safe money. Accumulated savings change a household's financial footing. Even if bad things don't happen we will capture more of our wealth potential by maintaining high savings and liquidity throughout our financial model.

External Rates of Return

An external rate of return is an internal rate of return, modified to account for values created by factors that are external to the vehicle producing the return, but which would not be present without that vehicle.

Imagine a restaurant that sells hamburgers and fountain sodas. If the return on investment for the hamburger is twenty-five percent, and the fountain sodas return is seventy-five percent, we would be tempted to consider removing hamburgers from the menu until we realized that the hamburgers create the traffic that makes possible the fountain sodas returns. Some of the profitability of the soda would not exist without the hamburger.

Savings has multiple external rates of return.

Savings allows us to take advantage of efficiencies such as higher deductibles on auto, home, liability, and health insurance, and longer exclusion periods on disability and long term care insurance. When savings allows us to purchase high deductible health insurance plans we realize additional HSA tax efficiencies. Savings allows us to pay annual premiums instead of monthly, buy bulk instead of individually packaged, and buy high quality that will last, instead of junk that has been designed to fail. Savings can prevent inefficiencies created when we access the money we stored in illiquid places, such as tax penalties, access fees, deferred sales charges, and being forced to sell in down markets.

Savings allows us to exercise prudence and wisdom with every purchase, and provides the liquidity to buy in the most economically efficient manner available. Savings positions us to take advantage of opportunities as they present, such as when people who lack savings sell assets at low prices in order to generate liquidity.

Savings prevents the need to borrow money at interest.

It is here useful to offer the perspective that lenders are not in the business of lending money. When a lender believes a potential borrower will not possess the capital to repay a loan, the lender will refuse the loan. In a sense lenders are in the business of supplying liquidity to borrowers who do not currently possess it, because it hasn't yet been earned, saved, or kept liquid, and they are able to charge dearly because liquidity is immensely valuable.

The person who keeps monies immediately available never pays a usurer for access to them.

Combined:

The combination of a strong defense, which prevents costly economic setbacks, PLUS high efficiency, which eventually recaptures fifteen to twenty percent of household income otherwise lost to inefficiency, PLUS recaptured opportunity costs, are the highest return of savings.

It is not possible to calculate the total return of savings because the difference between a household with savings and one without is a difference of kind, not degree. What is the percentage difference between healthy and diseased? What is the value of being one's own economic master?

Conversely, persons with little financial cushion often feel "pressed for money." They tend to buy failure-prone vehicles and appliances because they can be obtained cheaply and will suffice for the short term. When breakdowns occur, day to day living forces them to seek liquidity, often at high cost.

Persons with little financial cushion pay insurance premiums monthly instead of annually. They have low deductibles, and pay more for their insurance because they ask their insurance carriers to cover small, frequent losses. They sometimes feel forced to float checks, flirting with late fees and penalties. They buy on credit to capture "rewards," but often lose those rewards when they fail to make timely payments. They put money into risk assets with government penalties for early withdrawal, and then pay those penalties when unemployment strikes. They use credit to maintain lifestyle when their economic circumstances change. They buy on credit today based on tomorrow's windfall. When something prevents tomorrow's windfall, they witness the miracle of compound interest, fees, and charges, all in the red. What begins as a bad idea becomes a disaster that requires years to work off.

When something bad happens, which would otherwise be absorbed by liquid savings, they turn to lenders and from that point forward, much of the capital that should have been allocated to savings is siphoned off to pay interest. They lose all of the efficiencies and gains they could have earned with that money. They lose the optimism and security, the boldness in decision-making that a sound personal economy would have provided. They sense they have limited options and feel frustration knowing their best labor is building someone else's wealth. They then join the ranks of those hopeless souls who can only imagine a way forward if it is given to them in the form of some windfall, so they swing into the convenience store to participate in a voluntary tax on hopelessness. They buy a lottery ticket.

Imagine the woman who saves fifteen percent of every dollar she earns, starting with her first part time employment. Personal savings cushions against financial setbacks, allows adequate capital to flow into risk transference, and allows for less risk-taking in growth assets, **while accumulating greater wealth than is likely through low savings, low efficiency, and high risk.** She will never turn to a usurer for liquidity. She will finance larger purchases at rates reserved for the most credit worthy, or from her own reserves, whichever is the more efficient based on the circumstances. Her capital will allow her to make the best buying decision possible with every purchase she makes. She will not toil most of her life repaying debt masters. Much of the money that would have been lost to interest, penalties, fees, and pricing inefficiencies will instead grow in her accounts.

The highest return of savings is freedom. While a person whose household is built on debt and risk might behave as boldly as a person who follows sound economic principles—the first is as foolish as the latter is wise. The illusion of freedom is not freedom. Inevitably, life's surprises will make the former suffer, and the latter will quietly go about enjoying a life that to those on the outside looking in, appears charmed.

22 Stewardship

Genesis 2:15

And the LORD God took the man, and put him into the garden of Eden to dress it and to keep it.

Deuteronomy 10:14

Behold, the heaven and the heaven of heavens is the LORD's thy God, the earth also, with all that therein is.

1 Chronicles 29:11

Thine, O LORD is the greatness, and the power, and the glory, and the victory, and the majesty: for all that is in the heaven and in the earth is thine; thine is the kingdom, O LORD, and thou art exalted as head above all.

Psalm 50:10-12

For every beast of the forest is mine, and the cattle upon a thousand hills. I know all the fowls of the mountains: and the wild beasts of the field are mine. If I were hungry, I would not tell thee: for the world is mine, and the fulness thereof.

Matthew 25:14-30

For the kingdom of heaven is as a man travelling into a far country, who called his own servants, and delivered unto them his goods. And unto one he gave five talents, to another two, and to another one; to every man according to his several ability; and straightway took his journey. Then he that had received the five talents went and traded with the same, and made them other five talents. And likewise he that had received two, he also gained other two. But he that had received one went and digged in the earth, and hid his lord's money. After a long time the lord of those servants cometh, and reckoneth with them. And so he that had received five talents came and brought other five talents, saying, Lord, thou deliveredst unto me five talents: behold, I have gained beside them five talents more. His lord said unto him, Well done, thou good and faithful servant: thou hast been faithful over a few things, I will make thee ruler over many things: enter thou into the joy of thy lord. He also that had received two talents came and said, Lord, thou deliveredst unto me two talents: behold, I have gained two other talents beside them. His lord said unto him, Well done, good and faithful servant; thou hast been faithful over a few things, I will make thee ruler over many things: enter thou into the joy of thy lord. Then he which had received the one talent came and said, Lord, I knew thee that thou art an hard man, reaping where thou hast not sown, and gathering where thou hast not strawed: And I was afraid, and went and hid thy talent in the earth: lo, there thou hast that is thine. His lord answered and said unto him, Thou wicked and slothful servant, thou knewest that I reap where I sowed not, and gather where I have not strawed: Thou oughtest therefore to have put my money to the exchangers, and then at my coming I should have received mine own with usury. Take therefore the talent from him, and give it unto him which hath ten talents. For unto every one that hath shall be given, and he shall have abundance: but from him that hath not shall be taken away even that which he hath. And cast ye the unprofitable servant into outer darkness: there shall be weeping and gnashing of teeth.

Luke 12:42-44

And the Lord said, Who then is that faithful and wise steward, whom his lord shall make ruler over his household, to give them their portion of meat in due season? Blessed is that servant, whom his lord when he cometh shall find so doing. Of a truth I say unto you, that he will make him ruler over all that he hath.

Luke 12:47-48

And that servant, which knew his lord's will, and prepared not himself, neither did according to his will, shall be beaten with many stripes. But he that knew not, and did commit things worthy of stripes, shall be beaten with few stripes. For unto whomsoever much is given, of him shall be much required: and to whom men have committed much, of him they will ask the more.

Luke 16:9-11

And I say unto you, Make to yourselves friends of the mammon of unrighteousness; that, when ye fail, they may receive you into everlasting habitations. He that is faithful in that which is least is faithful also in much: and he that is unjust in the least is unjust also in much. If therefore ye have not been faithful in the unrighteous mammon, who will commit to your trust the true riches?

Romans 14:8

For whether we live, we live unto the Lord; and whether we die, we die unto the Lord: whether we live therefore, or die, we are the Lord's.

Commentary

In Genesis 2:15 the Lord put man in the Garden of Eden to cultivate and keep it. That sentence contains almost everything we need to understand about stewardship.

First, the Lord is the owner of both the man and the Garden.

Second, the Lord is the agent, the one with both authority and volition. The man is not choosing to go to the Garden because he connects with nature there. And his work within the Garden is not based on his interest in keeping it beautiful for future generations, or out of a desire to help protect the natural beauty he sees.

All of those might make sense, and it's a whole lot easier to do what the boss says when we agree with what he's trying to do. But the bottom line on stewardship is that the Lord places the man in the Garden for the Lord's purpose, not the man's, and that's the same as charging the man with an obligation.

Stewardship is a duty.

Third, left alone, the Garden of Eden would have unrealized potential. Occupied by a steward who dresses and keeps it, that potential is realized. Thus, the Lord expects more than the man's presence at the Garden. God didn't put him there to keep an eye on things. God expects output, work, the realization of potential.

Fourth, the Lord expects the man to keep the Garden, a word that encompasses many meanings. If we keep a pet, for example, we feed it, protect it, look after its health and smaller needs—in short, we accept an all-encompassing responsibility for its welfare. We anticipate its needs.

The concept of stewardship is tied to three recurring themes: God is sovereign, man and woman were built to work, and we are commanded to love one another.

When we act as stewards, we are to be guided by our best understanding of the Lord's wishes. When Jesus says in the parable of the talents,

> You wicked, lazy slave, you knew that I reap
> where I did not sow and gather where I scattered no
> seed. Then you ought to have put my money in the
> bank... --Matthew 25:26

He is saying the servant should have anticipated his master's wants and treated them as his duty.

This is more explicit in Luke 12:47,

> And that slave who knew his master's will and did
> not get ready or act in accord with his will, will re-
> ceive many lashes..."

Last, being faithful to the Lord isn't a function of how much the Lord has entrusted to us. It isn't about our social position, or our wealth. We don't have the latitude to be faithful in some areas and unfaithful in others which we feel are less important.

As we read in Luke 16: 10,

> "He that is faithful in a very little is faithful also in
> much: and he that is unrighteous in a very little is un-
> righteous also in much."

23 Success

Deuteronomy 30:9

And the Lord thy God will make thee plenteous in every work of thine hand, in the fruit of thy body, and in the fruit of thy cattle, and in the fruit of thy land, for good: for the Lord will again rejoice over thee for good, as he rejoiced over thy fathers.

Joshua 1:8

This book of the law shall not depart out of thy mouth; but thou shalt meditate therein day and night, that thou mayest observe to do according to all that is written therein: for then thou shalt make thy way prosperous, and then thou shalt have good success.

Nehemiah 2:20

Then answered I them, and said unto them, The God of heaven, he will prosper us; therefore we his servants will arise and build: but ye have no portion, nor right, nor memorial, in Jerusalem.

Psalm 1:1-3

Blessed is the man that walketh not in the counsel of the ungodly, nor standeth in the way of sinners, nor sitteth in the seat of the scornful. But his delight is in the law of the Lord; and in his law doth he meditate day and night. And he shall be like a tree planted by the rivers of water, that bringeth forth his fruit in his season; his leaf also shall not wither; and whatsoever he doeth shall prosper.

Psalm 37:4

Delight thyself also in the Lord: and he shall give thee the desires of thine heart.

Proverbs 22:29

Seest thou a man diligent in his business? he shall stand before kings; he shall not stand before mean men.

Proverbs 22:4

By humility and the fear of the Lord are riches, and honour, and life.

Isaiah 1:19

If ye be willing and obedient, ye shall eat the good of the land.

Matthew 6:24

No man can serve two masters: for either he will hate the one, and love the other; or else he will hold to the one, and despise the other. Ye cannot serve God and mammon.

Matthew 23:12

And whosoever shall exalt himself shall be abased; and he that shall humble himself shall be exalted.

Luke 9:48

And said unto them, Whosoever shall receive this child in my name receiveth me: and whosoever shall receive me receiveth him that sent me: for he that is least among you all, the same shall be great.

Ephesians 3:20

Now unto him that is able to do exceeding abundantly above all that we ask or think, according to the power that worketh in us.

24 Surety (Co-Signing)

Proverbs 6:1-5

My son, if thou be surety for thy friend, if thou hast stricken thy hand with a stranger, Thou art snared with the words of thy mouth, thou art taken with the words of thy mouth. Do this now, my son, and deliver thyself, when thou art come into the hand of thy friend; go, humble thyself, and make sure thy friend. Give not sleep to thine eyes, nor slumber to thine eyelids. Deliver thyself as a roe from the hand of the hunter, and as a bird from the hand of the fowler.

Proverbs 11:15

He that is surety for a stranger shall smart for it: and he that hateth suretiship is sure.

Proverbs 17:18

A man void of understanding striketh hands, and becometh surety in the presence of his friend.

Proverbs 22:26-27

Be not thou one of them that strike hands, or of them that are sureties for debts. If thou hast nothing to pay, why should he take away thy bed from under thee?

Proverbs 27:13

Take his garment that is surety for a stranger, and take a pledge of him for a strange woman.

25   Taxes

Matthew 22:21

They say unto him, Caesar's. Then saith he unto them, Render therefore unto Caesar the things which are Caesar's; and unto God the things that are God's.

Romans 13:7

Render therefore to all their dues: tribute to whom tribute is due; custom to whom custom; fear to whom fear; honour to whom honour.

Nehemiah 5:15

But the former governors that had been before me were chargeable unto the people, and had taken of them bread and wine, beside forty shekels of silver; yea, even their servants bare rule over the people: but so did not I, because of the fear of God.

Joshua 16:10

And they drave not out the Canaanites that dwelt in Gezer: but the Canaanites dwell among the Ephraimites unto this day, and serve under tribute.

26 Tithing

Genesis 28:20-22

And Jacob vowed a vow, saying, If God will be with me, and will keep me in this way that I go, and will give me bread to eat, and raiment to put on, So that I come again to my father's house in peace; then shall the LORD be my God: And this stone, which I have set for a pillar, shall be God's house: and of all that thou shalt give me I will surely give the tenth unto thee.

Deuteronomy 14:22-23

Thou shalt truly tithe all the increase of thy seed, that the field bringeth forth year by year. And thou shalt eat before the LORD thy God, in the place which he shall choose to place his name there, the tithe of thy corn, of thy wine, and of thine oil, and the firstlings of thy herds and of thy flocks; that thou mayest learn to fear the LORD thy God always.

Exodus 23:19

The first of the firstfruits of thy land thou shalt bring into the house of the LORD thy God. Thou shalt not seethe a kid in his mother's milk.

Exodus 34:26

The first of the firstfruits of thy land thou shalt bring unto the house of the LORD thy God. Thou shalt not seethe a kid in his mother's milk.

Leviticus 27:30

And all the tithe of the land, whether of the seed of the land, or of the fruit of the tree, is the LORD's: it is holy unto the LORD.

Numbers 18:26

Thus speak unto the Levites, and say unto them, When ye take of the children of Israel the tithes which I have given you from them for your inheritance, then ye shall offer up an heave offering of it for the LORD, even a tenth part of the tithe.

Deuteronomy 14:28

At the end of three years thou shalt bring forth all the tithe of thine increase the same year, and shalt lay it up within thy gates:

Deuteronomy 26:12

When thou hast made an end of tithing all the tithes of thine increase the third year, which is the year of tithing, and hast given it unto the Levite, the stranger, the fatherless, and the widow, that they may eat within thy gates, and be filled;

2 Chronicles 31:5

And as soon as the commandment came abroad, the children of Israel brought in abundance the firstfruits of corn, wine, and oil, and honey, and of all the increase of the field; and the tithe of all things brought they in abundantly.

Nehemiah 10:38

And the priest the son of Aaron shall be with the Levites, when the Levites take tithes: and the Levites shall bring up the tithe of the tithes unto the house of our God, to the chambers, into the treasure house.

Ezekiel 44:30

And the first of all the firstfruits of all things, and every oblation of all, of every sort of your oblations, shall be the priest's: ye shall also give unto the priest the first of your dough, that he may cause the blessing to rest in thine house.

Malachi 3:8-10

Will a man rob God? Yet ye have robbed me. But ye say, Wherein have we robbed thee? In tithes and offerings. Ye are cursed with a curse: for ye have robbed me, even this whole nation. Bring ye all the tithes into the storehouse, that there may be meat in mine house, and prove me now herewith, saith the LORD of hosts, if I will not open you the windows of heaven, and pour you out a blessing, that there shall not be room enough to receive it.

Matthew 23:23

Woe unto you, scribes and Pharisees, hypocrites! for ye pay tithe of mint and anise and cummin, and have omitted the weightier matters of the law, judgment, mercy, and faith: these ought ye to have done, and not to leave the other undone.

1 Corinthians 16:1-2

Now concerning the collection for the saints, as I have given order to the churches of Galatia, even so do ye. Upon the first day of the week let every one of you lay by him in store, as God hath prospered him, that there be no gatherings when I come.

Hebrews 7:1-4

For this Melchisedec, king of Salem, priest of the most high God, who met Abraham returning from the slaughter of the kings, and blessed him; To whom also Abraham gave a tenth part of all; first being by interpretation King of righteousness, and after that also King of Salem, which is, King of peace; Without father, without mother, without descent, having neither beginning of days, nor end of life; but made like unto the Son of God; abideth a priest continually. Now consider how great this man was, unto whom even the patriarch Abraham gave the tenth of the spoils.

Commentary

The subject of the tithe is delicate. The tithe was part of the Old Covenant, which began with Moses. The people agreed to keep the law and God promised to bless them in return. Moses received the Ten Commandments, which the people didn't keep for very long, ultimately resulting in the New Covenant established with Christ.

Under the New Covenant, when we have a relationship with Christ we have the indwelling Spirit of God guiding our works. Thus, a Christian is not under the Old Covenant, and is not required to tithe.

However, Hebrews 7: 1-4 (above) offers great illumination. The scripture recounts Abraham and Melchizedek, the King of Righteousness and the King of Peace, to whom Abraham gave a tenth of his choicest spoils.

Before Abraham, Cain, Abel and Job all made offerings, but the first mention of giving a tenth comes with Abraham in Genesis, 14:17-20, to which Hebrews 7: 1-4 refers.

> "...at the Valley of Shaveh (that is, the King's Valley), after his return from the defeat of Chedorlaomer and the kings who were with him. Then Melchizedek king of Salem brought out bread and wine; he was the priest of God Most High. And he blessed him and said: "Blessed be Abram of God Most High, Possessor of heaven and earth; And blessed be God Most High, who has delivered your enemies into your hand." And he gave him a tithe of all."

This is the first time the tithe is mentioned in the Bible, and it is noteworthy that the tithe was a tenth of the spoils Abraham took from a military victory over another people. Abraham didn't give a tenth of his overall possessions, but only of the spoils. Further, he gave freely, of his own will, and explicitly without expecting or wanting anything in return.

Abraham, of course, was not under the Old Covenant, and yet he gave back to the Lord. A similar example is found with Jacob in Genesis 28:20.

> "And Jacob vowed a vow, saying, If God will be with me, and will keep me in this way that I go, and will give me bread to eat, and raiment to put on, So that I come again to my father's house in peace; then shall the LORD be my God: And this stone, which I have set for a pillar, shall be God's house: and of all that thou shalt give me <u>I will surely give the tenth unto thee.</u>"

Again, this is a single occurrence of giving to the Lord.

Per 2 Chronicles 31:4-5, the tithe was established under the Old Covenant because of the weight of the priesthood and the official sacrificial system created to keep the people in the good graces of God.

> "Moreover he commanded the people who dwelt in Jerusalem to contribute support for the priests and the Levites, that they might devote themselves to the Law of the LORD. As soon as the commandment was circulated, the children of Israel brought in abundance the firstfruits of grain and wine, oil and honey, and of all the produce of the field; and they brought in abundantly the tithe of everything."

The rules for tithing found in the Old Covenant didn't exist four hundred years earlier when Abraham and Jacob gave to the Lord—even though each gave a tenth.

So while it is true that Christians are not bound by the Old Covenant—are they not instead bound by the same love of God, that same awe and appreciation for their Creator, that compelled Abraham and Jacob to give back to the Lord?

Everything in the Bible teaches the appropriate relationship between the created and their Creator. Just as having the presence of mind to begin a prayer by humbly recognizing the sovereignty and grace of God communicates something to Him, so does giving back freely of that which He has given you.

Look at the tithe not as a means to produce some sort of end, such as grace or favor, nor as an expression of obedience to a law you to which you are not bound. Instead, consider the tithe a free will expression of the reverence, gratefulness, and love you feel toward your Creator and Savior.

27 Work

Genesis 2:15

And the LORD God took the man, and put him into the garden of Eden to dress it and to keep it.

Exodus 23:12

Six days thou shalt do thy work, and on the seventh day thou shalt rest: that thine ox and thine ass may rest, and the son of thy handmaid, and the stranger, may be refreshed.

2 Chronicles 31:21

And in every work that he began in the service of the house of God, and in the law, and in the commandments, to seek his God, he did it with all his heart, and prospered.

Psalm 127:2

It is vain for you to rise up early, to sit up late, to eat the bread of sorrows: for so he giveth his beloved sleep.

Proverbs 10:4

He becometh poor that dealeth with a slack hand: but the hand of the diligent maketh rich.

Proverbs 12:14

A man shall be satisfied with good by the fruit of his mouth: and the recompence of a man's hands shall be rendered unto him.

Proverbs 12:24

The hand of the diligent shall bear rule: but the slothful shall be under tribute.

Proverbs 13:4

The soul of the sluggard desireth, and hath nothing: but the soul of the diligent shall be made fat.

Proverbs 13:11

Wealth gotten by vanity shall be diminished: but he that gathereth by labour shall increase.

Proverbs 14:23

In all labour there is profit: but the talk of the lips tendeth only to penury.

Proverbs 18:9

He also that is slothful in his work is brother to him that is a great waster.

Proverbs 20:4

The sluggard will not plow by reason of the cold; therefore shall he beg in harvest, and have nothing.

Proverbs 21:5

The thoughts of the diligent tend only to plenteousness; but of every one that is hasty only to want.

Proverbs 21:25

The desire of the slothful killeth him; for his hands refuse to labour.

Proverbs 22:29

Seest thou a man diligent in his business? he shall stand before kings; he shall not stand before mean men.

Proverbs 24:27

Prepare thy work without, and make it fit for thyself in the field; and afterwards build thine house.

Proverbs 24:30-34

I went by the field of the slothful, and by the vineyard of the man void of understanding; And, lo, it was all grown over with thorns, and nettles had covered the face thereof, and the stone wall thereof was broken down. Then I saw, and considered it well: I looked upon it, and received instruction. Yet a little sleep, a little slumber, a little folding of the hands to sleep: So shall thy poverty come as one that travelleth; and thy want as an armed man.

Proverbs 28:19

He that tilleth his land shall have plenty of bread: but he that followeth after vain persons shall have poverty enough.

Ecclesiastes 5:12

The sleep of a labouring man is sweet, whether he eat little or much: but the abundance of the rich will not suffer him to sleep.

Ecclesiastes 9:10

Whatsoever thy hand findeth to do, do it with thy might; for there is no work, nor device, nor knowledge, nor wisdom, in the grave, whither thou goest.

Ephesians 6:5-8

Servants, be obedient to them that are your masters according to the flesh, with fear and trembling, in singleness of your heart, as unto Christ; Not with eyeservice, as menpleasers; but as the servants of Christ, doing the will of God from the heart; With good will doing service, as to the Lord, and not to men: Knowing that whatsoever good thing any man doeth, the same shall he receive of the Lord, whether he be bond or free.

Colossians 3:23

And whatsoever ye do, do it heartily, as to the Lord, and not unto men;

1 Thessalonians 2:9

For ye remember, brethren, our labour and travail: for labouring night and day, because we would not be chargeable unto any of you, we preached unto you the gospel of God.

2 Thessalonians 3:10-11

For even when we were with you, this we commanded you, that if any would not work, neither should he eat. For we hear that there are some which walk among you disorderly, working not at all, but are busybodies.

1 Timothy 5:8

But if any provide not for his own, and specially for those of his own house, he hath denied the faith, and is worse than an infidel.

Hebrews 6:10

For God is not unrighteous to forget your work and labour of love, which ye have shewed toward his name, in that ye have ministered to the saints, and do minister.

Commentary

The first thing that happens in the entire Bible, which is the history of God and humankind, is that God rolls up his sleeves and creates something.

God takes resources that are only available to Him and builds something, our universe, our planet, everything. The first chapter of Genesis tells us how God made everything, and then after six days of work,

> And on the seventh day God ended his work which he had made; and he rested on the seventh day from all his work which he had made. –Genesis 2: 2

A lot of people read that and hear how important it is to rest. I think it's interesting that God worked six days out of seven. I doubt he pulled forty hour weeks.

I think Genesis starts with the very first lesson God has for humankind to learn. Just like a little boy or girl watches his mother or father and learns what to do. God makes it explicit in Exodus 23: 12.

> Six days thou shalt do thy work, and on the seventh day thou shalt rest.

Yes, it also says we're to rest on the seventh day, but the proportion of work to rest is pretty heavy. We're supposed to work a lot.

In Proverbs 13: 4 we see the consequences of both working and not working. The soul of the sluggard is filled with desire for things he or she can't have, but the soul of the diligent, the person who applies himself, shall be made fat. Making the soul fat is just another way of saying the soul will be satisfied. Or over-satisfied.

When Christ says you'll know a tree by its fruit, he's pointing out something we all recognize, that we are more defined by our work, what we do, than anything else. A motivational speaker I enjoy, Les Brown, gets to the point: You'll know a tree by its fruits. Not the fruit it talks about, or says it wants.

It's easy to say things. It's hard to do them.

Also, "the soul of the diligent being made fat" is saying that there is a natural satisfaction that comes from hard work. Ayn Rand, who wrote Atlas Shrugged, wrote that a person's highest sense of self comes from the work that he does.

God made us to enjoy work because it is integral to our survival. We were not born on a welfare planet, where God says we're all valuable, and because of that, he's going to plant the fields for us, tend the animals for us, and manufacture televisions for us, so we can relax all day. Consider Proverbs 20: 4:

> The sluggard will not plow by reason of the cold;
> therefore shall he beg in harvest, and have nothing.

So God tells us not to be consumed with worry, and to trust that He will provide—but also, that some of His provision might come in the form of another person who worked harder than us, taking pity on us when we beg.

When I read passages like *Consider the lilies*, my sense is that God wants us to have faith in the big picture. We're saved. In biggest sense, in the greatest battle, we've been saved from an absolutely certain loss, by the unmerited grace of God.

But that doesn't mean we don't have to participate in our own existence. We still have to survive in the world as He created it, where you go hungry if you don't work.

28 Worry

Isaiah 51:12

I, even I, am he that comforteth you: who art thou, that thou shouldest be afraid of a man that shall die, and of the son of man which shall be made as grass;

Matthew 6:25

Therefore I say unto you, Take no thought for your life, what ye shall eat, or what ye shall drink; nor yet for your body, what ye shall put on. Is not the life more than meat, and the body than raiment?

Matthew 6:31-33

Therefore take no thought, saying, What shall we eat? or, What shall we drink? or, Wherewithal shall we be clothed? (For after all these things do the Gentiles seek:) for your heavenly Father knoweth that ye have need of all these things. [33] But seek ye first the kingdom of God, and his righteousness; and all these things shall be added unto you.

Matthew 6:34

Take therefore no thought for the morrow: for the morrow shall take thought for the things of itself. Sufficient unto the day is the evil thereof.

Luke 12:22-29

And he said unto his disciples, Therefore I say unto you, Take no thought for your life, what ye shall eat; neither for the body, what ye shall put on. The life is more than meat, and the body is more than raiment. Consider the ravens: for they neither sow nor reap; which neither have storehouse nor barn; and God feedeth them: how much more are ye better than the fowls? And which of you with taking thought can add to his stature one cubit? If ye then be not able to do that thing which is least, why take ye thought for the rest? Consider the lilies how they grow: they toil not, they spin not; and yet I say unto you, that Solomon in all his glory was not arrayed like one of these. If then God so clothe the grass, which is to day in the field, and to morrow is cast into the oven; how much more will he clothe you, O ye of little faith? And seek not ye what ye shall eat, or what ye shall drink, neither be ye of doubtful mind.

Philippians 4:6

Be careful for nothing; but in every thing by prayer and supplication with thanksgiving let your requests be made known unto God.

Hebrews 13:6

So that we may boldly say, The Lord is my helper, and I will not fear what man shall do unto me.

1 Peter 5:7

Casting all your care upon him; for he careth for you.

CONCLUSION:

I n the financial planning world, legacy has to do with passing on things of value. This could be a business, or money that goes to heirs, or property. But the word legacy means more than that. If you think of your grandparent's legacy, do you automatically think about how much money they passed on? Or does legacy capture something bigger? Consider Deuteronomy 6: 5-7:

> And thou shalt love the Lord thy God with all thine heart, and with all thy soul, and with all thy might. And these words, which I command thee this day, shall be in thine heart: And thou shalt teach them diligently unto thy children, and shalt talk of them when thou sittest in thine house, and when thou walkest by the way, and when thou liest down, and when thou risest up.

In a holistic sense, Legacy means, how much of who you are, your values, your beliefs, your achievements, and your productivity... how much of that survives in the next generation. Your legacy might be wisdom that you've written in books or letters. It might be the fact that your children are good people because it was important to you to make them good people.

But legacy also has a financial sense. According to Proverbs 13:22:

> A good man leaveth an inheritance to his children's children: and the wealth of the sinner is laid up for the just.

This doesn't mean that God is saying to buy a big life insurance policy, although life insurance has a place in every sound financial plan.

The meaning of this proverb ties up neatly the meaning of this entire booklet. A good person leaves an inheritance not just to his children, but to his grandchildren.

Earlier I wrote that a faithful person isn't just a one who has faith, it's a person whose life evidences that faith. It's a person who demonstrates faith by living according to the advice God has given.

Here I read a "good man" the exact same way. If you recall all of the scriptures dealing with money, and the theology from the first half of this booklet, you know that we're to keep the LORD first in everything.

So is this proverb telling us that in order to be good we have to instead leave a huge amount of money to our families?

Not at all. In fact I read it as the exact opposite. That God created the world so that people who do right things will, overall, prosper greatly.

I read this to mean that a good person, who lives according to the rules, who puts God first, will inevitably create wealth that lasts for generations.

If we were to recap, then, the principles about money we've discussed:

- Work 6 days a week
- Be productive with your resources (Stewardship)

- Be intelligent about debt
- Save regularly, save a lot, and save with purpose
- Put your money to use, but take steps to mitigate risks

Do you think it's possible for a person in the United States to work six days a week for an entire career, saving a lot of money from each pay, avoiding bad forms of debt, and keeping assets productive, while mitigating risk… can you imagine that person not creating a substantial financial legacy?

> But seek ye first the kingdom of God, and his righteousness; and all these things shall be added unto you.   --Matthew 6: 33

I think the financial message in the Bible is a hopeful message, that when we put God first and live right, that the natural order of the way God created the universe is that things will be all right. All these things that will be added are the exact things we're told not to worry about.

AFTERWORD:

You might think that in this modern world of stock options, 401ks, mutual funds, adjustable rate mortgages, hedge funds, and all the myriad financial tools that exist, that it's impossible to run your financial house according to principles in the Bible, or that principles written more than two thousand years ago really aren't relevant today.

It happens that the principles in the Bible for dealing with money actually work. I've helped a lot of people with their finances and it's remarkable, but whenever I find mistakes that people are making, it always comes down to not following the principles we just reviewed.

In fact, if I was to categorize the mistakes I see most often, it's that folks save little, waste a lot, don't make full productive use of all either their time or their money, and take risks they don't understand when the do try to make their resources productive.

The bottom line is that you can trust the advice the Bible gives about money.

For me, it's exhilarating to help people using these principles. I've found that these principles have the ability to right a household's finances, improve standards of living, create wealth and extend legacies.

The financial principles in the Bible allow us to live up to our highest ideals as human beings, as protectors and providers for the people who depend upon us.

You should trust what the Bible says about money.

I met a woman at a *LORD and Money* seminar I delivered at a church. She slowed in her car with the window rolled down as I walked to my Jeep, and said the Lord had told her she would be rich. I met with her later to see if I could be of counsel, and learned her financial life was in ruin, and that she would never be rich without a miracle, or a profound change in the way she thought about money. The amazing thing, however, was that she was a child of Christ in every way that would be obvious to measure. She gave of her time and her money. She was devout in her faith. She talked to the Lord all the time, consorted with Christians and tried to use her energy and her resources to bless other people. But her financial life was rock solid evidence that she'd never read or taken to account the Bible's wisdom on money, and that without Godly advice on money, she would likely never escape the misery and chains she'd created for herself.

> There were those who dwelt in darkness and in the shadow of death, prisoners in misery and chains, because they had rebelled against the words of God, and spurned the counsel of the Most High. Therefore He humbled their heart with labor. --Psalm 107: 10-12

Like Psalm 107: 10-12, the consequences of failing to heed God's advice was that her life was a series of financial mishaps. Instead of working because she loved to bless others and wax strong in the strength God gave her, she worked three jobs in near desperation, kiting checks, buying merchandise for her store with title loans and high interest credit cards, and praying for a miracle.

I see it in my professional life as a financial planner every day. It's almost as we think the Bible is only about spiritual matters, and has nothing of consequence to say about life in the flesh. Bills. Trust. Obligations. Resources. After all, it's not like the Bible was written after the invention of 401ks or 15 year mortgages. So most of the folks I meet have chosen to take the world's, and not God's, advice on money.

Which is probably why so many resemble those in Psalm 107:

> ...prisoners in misery and chains because they had rebelled against the words of God, and spurned the counsel of the Most High.

They look at me sheepishly, ashamed, and try to make me understand why they have saved so little. It's always rational. Any person would make the same decisions—because no one chooses to do foolish things. We all try to choose the higher value. It's just that sometimes what we value higher is not what God tells us to. Sometimes we value our pride, our comfort, or enabling someone who is using us as a financial resource, more than the principles God gives us.

Yet, while some people are enslaved in debt and the never-ending consequences of bad decisions, others can take those same resources and experiences and turn them into a life of bounty. Of the two, which do you think is more capable of blessing others as God would have us do?

The Bible tells us to do several things which, added up, work with perfect logic and lead to economic health:

- Work 6 days out of 7
- Live within your means
- Save A Lot, with purpose
- Be a Good Steward (make your resources productive)
- Mitigate Risk, and
- Only use productive debt, and then do so sparingly

But before you can really own those principles, meaning, know them and live them, several things have to happen.

First, you have to accept Christ into your life and receive the Holy Spirit. My personal belief is that coming to these principles without having the Holy Spirit to guide you in their application to your life is almost like finding a Rosetta stone–for languages you don't speak. So first, get right with God. Read up on as much apologetics as you have to, but there's no excuse for not believing in Christ. There's simply no way to get around the historical fact that He lived, died, and was resurrected–and if you discount that statement, you simply haven't studied the matter. Read Mike Licona, William Lane Craig, or Lee Strobel for starters.

Second, you have to let the Lord transform you into a new being by changing the way you think. Over time, the Holy Spirit teaches you and transforms you into a new being. When this happens, when you read the Bible you're illuminated with wisdom designed just for you, whatever place you are at. You care about different things and your thoughts change.

Third, in order to deeply apply the principles above, you either need to be a financial expert with the resources to test ideas, or you need to take counsel from someone who is. The reason is that the financial world is complicated, and what the Bible tells you to do with money stands in direct contrast to what most financial salespeople will tell you to do with your money, and also in contrast to the information most of the financial press provides (because they often cater to high risk). So if you're going to go it alone, you should know that almost all purveyors of retail financial information are there to guide you into their products, and your instincts, groomed by the culture you've grown up in, are quite possibly going to work against you.

If you decide to seek counsel, you should also know that most of the people working in financial services are working for their own purposes first, their company's second, and yours, third. This isn't because they are trying to take advantage of you. It's because they're operating a business and need to be profitable, and their only ally is the company that's teaching them how to sell financial products.

Bottom line is that you need to find counsel from people of like mind but deeper experience. The first place to find this counsel is the Holy Spirit. The second is the Bible. The third is your financial planner.

ACCEPTING COUNSEL

Three (related) things get in the way of accepting God's counsel.

We want to keep God out of certain areas of our lives where we want to remain unholy–but human and happy

Hubris or shame keeps us from admitting that we need God's counsel in certain areas.

We turn to worldly advice instead of Godly advice. Almost like Socrates said: we choose our advice when we choose our advisor.

> Many are the plans in a man's heart, but the counsel of the Lord, it will stand.   Psalm 33:10-11

Every time I read this I can't escape the thought that man's mind is tiny, his maps of the universe incomplete, one-dimensional, penned as much in prejudice as ink. And as much as man pores over the contours of the world he believes is real, and believes the fictions he calls physical laws, he has barely any hope of navigating life safely. Meanwhile the Creator of the Universe tells him exactly how to avoid the dangers and tragedies, and man does nothing. As if he hasn't even read the words.

Of course, we have a vested interest in not registering the meanings behind the words. God wants us to be holy and we love our vices. Hey, this is my vice. It's my only one. My only *big* one. I'll keep this to myself and as long as I go to church and say "GREAT!!!" when people ask me how I'm doing, all's good. God isn't meant to be everywhere.

Yet keeping God out of our finances only leads to a distorted household cash flow system, whereby, because we prefer to consume today instead of saving for tomorrow, we end up siphoning off vast amounts of our future recourses to debt service. The ultimate irony is that the person who prefers to consume to-day gets to consume much less over time than the person who prefers to save.

The next reason I think we avoid God's counsel is that we're arrogant. God's largely silent and we're in control anyway. Consider Saul:

> So Saul died for his trespass which he committed against the Lord, because of the word of the Lord which he did not keep; and also because he asked counsel of a medium, making inquiry of it, and did not inquire of the Lord. Therefore He [God] killed him [Saul], and turned the kingdom to David the son of Jesse. --1 Chronicles 10:13-14

Why did Saul consult a medium? Samuel, who is actually dead and summoned by the medium mentioned in Chronicles above, tells Saul:

> The Lord has done just as he said he would. He has taken the kingdom from you and given it to your rival, David. The LORD has done this because you did not obey his instructions concerning the Amalekites. --1 Samuel 28:17

Peeling back the onion further, why did Saul ignore the Lord's instructions regarding the Amalekites? 1 Samuel 15 explains: Samuel relayed instructions from the Lord to Saul. The Lord was settling accounts with the Amalekites for opposing Israel when they came from Egypt. Saul was to destroy the Amalekite nation–the men, women, children, babies, cattle, sheep, camels, and donkeys. What did Saul do? He destroyed everything but the king, which he kept as a kind of trophy, and some of the livestock which allowed his men to keep as plunder.

So to put this in context, God made Saul king, gave him explicit directions, and Saul carried them out not as if he was fulfilling a charge, but as if he was acting on his own behalf, with his own satisfaction as the highest end.

The result? The Lord rejected Saul.

Yeah, but those times were different. God expects more of a king. And that was Old Testament stuff. Christians don't even need the Old Testament. Dude, God is forgiveness and love...

Yet, the New Testament tells us that with the New Covenant we have the indwelling Spirit of God, guiding us. And that a follower of Christ is transformed in his thoughts, and becomes a new person. So it seems that the lesson of Saul, though harsh, is still applicable. If we are Christians, we are to be growing, listening to God's counsel, reading his word and applying his advice to our lives. We don't get to carve out areas where we disobey–at least not where we've been given explicit instructions.

But that leaves a giant gray area, doesn't it? In fact, we don't have very many explicit instructions. Just the Ten Commandments and Christ telling us to love one another. So what about the areas where we don't actually *need* God's advice? Or those difficult areas where, because the Bible was written so long ago, there's no direct advice? Areas where God's stance seems so... old fashioned and uninformed.

If you listen closely you'll hear the same refrain as the other objections. I'm a man and the last thing I want to do is roll the window down and ask someone how to get to where I'm going. Yes, I'm confused, but I'd rather make mistakes, get lost, and waste a lot of time and gas. I'd gladly suffer *those* consequences over the shame of looking another man in the eye and allowing him to know I'm lost. Because somewhere in my upbringing I learned that real men know where they are and how to get where they're going. Part of our self-respect comes from our ability to navigate our lives.

Same thing with money–it's like we're all aware of a standard we're not living up to, so we'd rather deal with the setbacks alone than allow someone else to know how far we've missed the targets we believe we should have hit.

> The way of a fool is right in his own eyes, but a
> wise man is he who listens to counsel. --Proverbs 12:15

What does all this have to do with accepting God's advice on money? First, we don't get to choose to follow some advice and ignore other advice. Sure, we can, but there are consequences. The consequences for Saul were his death and loss of kingdom. The consequences to us, financially, are that we live in dark desperation, one paycheck from disaster, shackled to bad decisions we made years ago, and hopeless that we'll ever break free.

Putting God's Counsel into Effect

So how do we accept God's advice on money? First, accept God. If Christ isn't your savior, you don't have the Holy Spirit, and you're not going to do very well trying to follow the Bible. Once you have the Holy Spirit, then read the Bible and listen for insight. You'll find the Bible has 2300 verses on money, so there's wisdom in every context.

Principles are value-based rules that are generally true. Pull your principles from the Bible, and think about them enough to decide which to give the heavier weight. A big part of maturing as a human being is learning which values are primary and which are secondary, so we know not only what is good, but what is better. In decisions where we have to choose between competing values, which is most decisions, having thought through the weight of our principles will enable us to choose what represents the greater value. Such as, giving a man a fish is a good thing.... but teaching him to fish is a greater thing.

The principles mentioned above are:
- Work 6 days out of 7
- Live within your means
- Save A Lot, with purpose
- Be a Good Steward (make your resources productive)
- Mitigate Risk, and
- Only use productive debt, sparingly

These are the most basic financial rules in the Bible. But how do you actually apply them in modern life? How do these rules help you understand whether it's better to put money into your 401k, where you'll get a small match, or to pay off a credit card?

Because there is an underlying hierarchy of values.

All of the principles above can be organized around the idea of stewardship, or being a productive with the resources we've been given. Everything in your financial life can be weighed from that standpoint. In fact, most everyone has heard of "opportunity cost." That's just a way of expressing whether one use of a resource is more productive than another.

Think about the above principles holistically, weighed from a perspective of good stewardship and productivity. Doesn't it lead to a self-evidently obvious healthy household finance system? You are productive, create value, and earn money. Because you live within your means you are able to save money, which keeps you from paying debt interest, keeping not just you productive, but your resources as well. When you mitigate risk, you prevent mishaps from derailing your productivity and your money's. And when you only use productive debt, you limit the financial drag of usury, which in turn keeps your resources more productive.

Once the principles are in place, it still makes sense to seek counsel.

> Or what king, when he sets out to meet another
> king in battle, will not firth sit down and take counsel
> whether he is strong enough with ten thousand men
> to encounter the one coming against him with twenty
> thousand?   --Luke 13:31

I know Luke wasn't writing about the modern notion of retirement, but reading Luke 13:31, I can't help but think of the challenges facing people who are looking forward to retiring in the next ten to twenty years.

I say this because the army of twenty thousand that you're going to be doing battle with is a mean army, well stocked, and full of surprises. Social Security is funded worse than Detroit's pension system. Our national debt to GDP is 105%, meaning we can expect slower growth. We have negative real interest rates, which wherever that has happened in the world, has led to much poorer equity and bond performance. We have stock markets seemingly poised for another massive correction, this after having had two 50% downward movements in the last 14 years. We have inflation set to increase rapidly, and a government so deeply in debt we can't help but to expect rising taxes. Retirees must face all of that and figure out how to create income streams that will increase when interest rates increase, but not be subject to our nation's bubble financial markets' volatility.

So do seek counsel. The principles get you started, but really what you should use them for is to build a worldview that serves as a litmus test for your advisors. Meaning, don't take advice from people who don't also share the tenets of your belief system. Or if they differ, be aware of where they differ so you can evaluate their advice from an informed point of view.

Don't be the guy who can't ask for directions.

There are solutions to the problems posed by the army of twenty thousand. God's principles, and advice from godly advisors, will get you through.

About the Author

Clayton Lindemuth CLU ChFC is a financial planner in Chesterfield, Missouri, where he lives with his wife Julie and their dog, Faith.

His hobbies include ultra-distance running, backpacking, writing, and economics.

He may be reached at clayton@pathfinderadvocates.com, or

37713936R00102

Made in the USA
Charleston, SC
18 January 2015